£5.50

GIUSEPPE
DE LOGU
MARIO ABIS

THE GOLDEN CENTURIES OF VENETIAN PAINTING

Original title:
A VELENCEI FESTÉSZET FÉNYKORA
Corvina, Budapest, 1975

Translated by
LILI HALÁPY and TAMÁS HARASTY
Translation revised by
E. GEORGE MADDOCKS

Photographs:
from the archives of Corvina Press (by Alfréd Schiller):
Nos. 1, 11, 18, 20, 21, 22, 35, 39, 45
Alinari, Florence: Nos. 8, 9, 13, 14, 27, 28
Feruzzi, Venice: Nos. 29, 36, 46
Giraudon, Paris: Nos. 23, 37, 40
Kunsthistorisches Museum, Vienna: No. 2
National Gallery, Washington: Nos. 5, 6
Scala, Florence: Nos. 3, 4, 7, 10, 12, 15, 16, 17, 19, 24, 25,
26, 30, 31, 32, 33, 34, 38, 41, 42, 43, 44, 47, 48

Description of Plates 40 and 41 by Ildikó Ember

It needs rashness, rather than courage, to attempt to introduce, however briefly, and to describe things that our eyes can barely touch and that we can only really approach with our hearts and our minds. It is such things that make up the history of Venice—a history which the power of sight turns into poetry.

Titian called his own paintings "poems". In his last years Goethe, overwhelmed by his desire for painting, and evidently having *his* Venice in mind, rhapsodised in his *Conversations* from Weimar: "Painters are the gods of the earth—a poet is nothing!"

After these late reflexions of Goethe it is worth reading what he wrote when he first set eyes on Venice: ". . .For it had been ordained on my page in the Book of Destiny that I should see Venice first in the evening, at five o'clock our time, on the 28th September, 1786, sailing from the Brenta into the Lagoon; not long afterwards I was able to set foot on the soil of this marvellous city of islands, this beaver republic, and to spend some time there. Thus, thank God, Venice is for me no longer a mere word, a meaningless name, one that had so often terrified me, so mortal am I an enemy of flowery rhetoric. . ." *(Italian Journey)*. And the next day, the 29th September, the great courtier recorded: "Everything that surrounds me is majestic, the creation of persistent human efforts, the magnificent and outstanding achievement, not of one ruler but of a whole people."

In the beginning this creation was a vocation, which later grew into a mission: from being merely the idiom of the Veneto these colours, this painting became a universal language, understood in Madrid and London, Vienna, Warsaw, Augsburg and Dresden.

By representing the most interesting episodes in the history and workaday life of Venice, Venetian painting turned material and human decline into eternal glory. And not even the frequent wars and other adversities, not even looting and speculating and the removal of so many works of art could make this unique and invaluable heritage vanish. So much so that as early as 1660 Marco Boschini (1613–1678) in his work *La Carta del navegar pittoresco* [Map of Pictorial Navigation] was able to state:

> *All our great buildings will crumble to dust*
> . . . .
> *And the world, time and death together*
> *Will vanquish us, miserable mortals;*
> *We shall depart—but painting will live on.*

The same poet-critic avers that the history of Venice can be told by means of painting, which is

> *. . . a brilliant mirror*
> *Spacious enough to hold the entire world.*

Here, to quote Taine's words, ". . . the eye could feel itself the colours' artist", and here, as Diego Valeri said, "Everything becomes painting and from everything a picture is born." Thus one, basing his views on nature, climate and the surroundings, the other, with a purely poetic interpretation, agree that ". . . such painting can only be born, and live, in Venice: it is wholly imbued with the Venetian spirit, a spirit which at first only hovered above the dried-out beds of the lagoons, but finally donned the forms of a city and became Venice, the city that has no walls, the very realization of colour". Here colour becomes a manifestation of the spirit and reigns over Art as mother, priestess and teacher. But when they are embodied in painting, colours become the expression, the synonym of what we mean by the word "Venetian": the art of colour in poetry, the *colore*, colour in the theatre, the overall effect of colour, the famous *coloratura* in music, and colour even in sculptures and buildings, not as though multicoloured marble was used, but because they seem 6 to feel the possibilities offered by tones and velvety *chiaroscuro*. That is why Fiocco calls Venice *Urbs picta*; that is why Michelangelo perceived that "this whole city"—with its palaces, lagoons and canals, with its crystal-clear sky, now veiled, now dazzling—"is a magnificent painting". While Michelangelo remarked that in Venice there were vast numbers of good pictures, two centuries later, on the 14th August 1739, De Brosses stated: "The y say that in Venice there are more paintings than in the whole o Italy. As far as I am concerned, I may well say that there are more pictures here than in the whole of France." It is colour that expresses both the appearance and the essence of everything. Colour "reflects and can hold" the whole world; it is the language that contains the whole of Venetian history, which, according to Charles Diehl, the great Byzantinologist, "is the supreme example in history of active energy and of the practical use of such energy".

A final piece of evidence of this view is the survival of Venetian painting, which has left us an unequalled and animated picture of the city. As early as the dawn of Venetian civilization, colour was a clearly identifiable part of the tradition handed down from the Orient, where it was first manifested in the golden glimmer of mosaic. Towards the sunset of that civilization it was transformed into the peculiar lyrical universality of the eighteenth century, the period of enlightenment, into Tiepolo's airy panoramas and his ceiling-paintings of heaven; into crystal-like *vedute*, those last novelties of Venetian art, which enriched not only Venice, but Dresden, London, Vienna and Warsaw as well, with splendid, archaic townscapes. In them, Venetian painting became Francesco Guardi's *perpetuum mobile*, an eternal and miraculous reflection of a benevolent *fata morgana*.

Thus the antecedents of Venetian painting can be found in the art of mosaics; Oriental tastes passed through Ravenna, which was under Byzantine rule, and then took root in the lagoons.

It was in mosaics that the Venetians found a way of satisfying their love of luxury and colour. In the eleventh and twelfth centuries they were still inviting Byzantine masters from the Orient to begin the marvellous mosaics in St. Mark's; but in the thirteenth and fourteenth centuries it was local masters who continued the work. Owing to their Latin upbringing and tradition, they gradually grew further and further away from Byzantine stylisation and drew their inspiration from more human and natural forms. Finally they reached the spirit of the Romanesque and Gothic styles.

The independence gained by Venice and her artistic culture indicate the break between the decline of the art of mosaics and the beginnings of mural and easel painting. But up to the late fifteenth century there was no genuine Venetian painting. In the fourteenth and fifteenth centuries sculpture and architecture flourished in an individual manner. Their intimate, charming and subtle creations prepared the ground for the invention of *vedutas*. But the great moment for painting was the day in 1408 when Gentile da Fabriano cast anchor in the lagoon. In his "flamboyant Gothic" art strange movements and feelings were sprouting and the inspiration of delicate, fairy-tale-like poetry made itself felt. This art revealed the artist's Umbrian and Sienese training, as well as the effect of Lombard and French art. In the Doges' Palace Gentile gave a foretaste of historic painting and his work as a portraitist bore witness to his realist approach.

Fabriano's works grafted a new effect on the budding tree of Venetian painting. Only Antonello's stay there sixty years later can be compared to them in significance. The style and exquisite poetic qualities of Fabriano's œuvre enthralled the nobler minds of the period; they accepted his encouragement without any hesitation. The most outstanding among them was Pisanello, the most faithful Jacopo Bellini.

There can be no doubt that the golden age of Venetian painting began with the Bellini dynasty. In honour of his master, Jacopo had his son baptised Gentile. Gentile Bellini was one year older than his brother Giovanni, or Giambellino, who grew into a patriarch of painting and who sealed the brotherly love between them by completing the canvas *St. Mark's Sermon in Alexandria*, which Gentile had left unfinished in 1507.

This Gentile was also a member of the group called the "narrative" artists. The creations of these painters are indeed precious. They were witty observers of moral and material customs and, under the pretext of praising holy days, processions or religious legends, they produced such intimate or majestic cycles as the *Legend of St. Ursula* (Vittore Carpaccio), or the *Legend of the Relics of the Holy Cross*. This latter used to be in the Scuola Grande di San Giovanni Evangelista, the edifice belonging to the Brotherhood of St. John the Evangelist, and is at present displayed at the Accademia in Venice. In these ventures lesser artists, such as Mansueti and Diana, worked together with Gentile Bellini and with Carpaccio (Plate 7). And though he was a Venetian, Gentile was daring enough also to represent exotic Oriental visions.

Meanwhile, however, newer painters with greater influence also came together in Venice: the Florentines Filippo Lippi and Paolo Uccello stayed here (the latter from 1426 to 1432); Andrea del Castagno worked in the Church of San Zaccaria in 1442. The most significant among them was Antonello da Messina, a singular, strange genius. He stayed in Venice from 1475 to 1476 and these two years were enough to turn him from a Sicilian into a Venetian and thus to make him eligible to be admitted to this selected company, to such an extent that even today it is argued whether he gave or received more. There have been attempts to belittle the power of his inspiration in order to emphasize even more strongly the undoubtedly immeasurable merits of the great Tuscan artist Piero della Francesca. However this may be, it is a fact that both of them had a deep effect on the art of the mature Giambellino. It has been said of the altar-piece of San Cassiano—which reveals the effect of sunny Sicily, though somewhat muted by Venetian colourism—that the unity of scenes in the great altar-pieces of the Venetians can be traced back to this picture (Plate 2).

Local traditions, help from Tuscany, Piero della Francesca and Mantegna from Padua—all encouraged the now aging Giambellino, in the last twenty years of the century, to change his approach to emphasizing linear qualities (the second *Transfiguration* in Naples), and, by decreasing the significance of formal beauty (*The Allegory of Souls in Purgatory*, Florence; Plate 4), to reach, by way of the triptych of the Church of the Frari,

9

the altar-piece of the Venetian Church of San Giovanni Crisostomo, which is considered by many scholars to be a break-through into a new period.

On the 7th February 1506 Albrecht Dürer wrote: "... He is very old and still the best in painting." The great Nuremberg master saw what was happening: namely that a group of pupils and imitators had come into being around Giambellino, and even that the course of the first glorious period of Venetian painting had been clearly demarcated. He was also in close contact with the greatest painters: Jacopo Palma (Palma Vecchio) and Titian, and even Giorgione, who died in 1510. This was six years before the death of Giovanni Bellini, whose pupil he had been. He overshadowed his master's fame and created by his œuvre a holy mystery which even today disturbs and disquiets the thinking of art philosophers, the wisdom of historians and the soul of connoisseurs. It is by no means due to chance that the *Feast of the Gods* (Washington; Plates 5–6), which is perhaps Bellini's last work, is a revelation. Not only and not so much on account of the new manner of representation, absolutely profane, even overtly mythological and pagan, but also because this work, which Bellini left unfinished because of his age, was, according to tradition, completed by Titian. That is why R. Longhi declared that "without wincing it tolerates Titian's thundering landscape as its completion".

But one thing is true, whether Titian finished the *Feast of the Gods* or only saw it, he pursued its inspiration in his pictures representing merry-making or festivals of Venus, which date from exactly the same time. Just when Giambellino's renewed world concept reached its final triumph, Titian's opened to a new life; this was not long after Giorgione had immortalized his own world concept in the undying blaze of light which made his lightning-brilliant landscape and his *Sleeping Venus* so ravishing. It is a fact of historic importance that Tiziano Vecellio took a hand in the work of a great master; for, although questions of stylistic and morphological attributions may arise, the deed was evidence of a spiritual unity and justified the endeavours that enabled Titian to wield his brush in the works of Bellini, Palma or Giorgione. This meant that Venetian painting, with 10 its distinctive characteristics, had appeared on the scene, and now set out on a wonderful course of development.

It is surprising how Giambellino reached this maturity; the belated painter of Madonnas started by copying his father's example. Then he transformed his representations of the Virgin and Child into an interpretation, wistful and yet in advance of his time, of the first secrets of life. He left behind ecclesiastical, devotional pictures and created from the theme a genuine poem of motherhood (Plate 3).

Thus it was in Bellini's workshop that the three greatest personages of Venetian painting in the first half of the sixteenth century, Giorgione, Palma Vecchio and Titian, were reared. Though the figure of Giorgio da Castelfranco lived on for over thirty years after his death in 1510, Titian, thanks to his inexhaustible intuition, to the freshness of his creative powers, renewed decade after decade, to his long life, and thanks to the vigour and lyricism of his art, not only became the most prominent personality of the century but also one of the supreme personalities of the universal history of painting. If Giambellino was the patriarch of Venetian painting, Titian became its Apollo; he is the greatest figure of Venetian and Italian painting.

The idea of a "transition" from one period to another between the fifteenth and sixteenth centuries seems to be groundless or arbitrary, since the new century was so completely new. This novelty was represented, first of all, by Giorgione (Giorgio da Castelfranco, *c.* 1477–1510). Although, as early as the beginning of the sixteenth century, the literature about him would have filled a whole library, he was a wholly mysterious personality. His training and the fact that it was Bellini who introduced him to the secrets of drawing, are probable and acceptable but by no means satisfying explanation for all the innovations of his art.

The effect of Leonardo da Vinci to be discerned in Giorgione's works has been often noted; the explanation is obvious: from the end of December 1499 Leonardo stayed in Venice. In two paintings by Giorgione traces of this influence are said to be found *(Boy with Arrow* and *Shepherd with Flute)*, and it is stressed that the application of "darkness", or of half-light, bears witness to identical principles and to a mutual affinity. However, in Leonardo's intellectual world the ideas of painting were brought into harmony with a scientific and philosophical system. It was in painting that his vocation and his intuition found their only possible form in which he could express his understanding and knowledge of nature; in his œuvre the lyricism of art, the certainty of science and the truth of philosophy are united.

There is less of the philosopher's struggle and meditation in Giorgione's art, which is characterized by intimacy of vision and emotion, and by the deeply spiritual quality of his painting. This does not try to surpass its subject, either in light or in colour. Giorgione loved nature as much as he loved turning nature into art; in his works the emotional elements of nature vibrate and there is a tension hidden in the divine calmness of forms and in the magic of light. The vagueness characteristic of Leonardo da Vinci springs, with Giorgione, from an innate sense of tones and therefore the "darkness"-conveying shade is realized by subtle modulations of light, shade and semi-obscurity.

Nature enchanted Giorgione, who lacked the anguish, the curiosity and the terror that excited Leonardo's mind whenever he was confronted with the microcosm which always seemed to him full of mystery. For Giorgione the world, which he viewed as though in a dream, became through colour his poetry and his music. In his world, which is shown to us by the very few works which were incontestably produced by his brush, there are no breaks and no signs of dualism. In vain did the critics' Sisyphus-like labours swell the catalogues with works assigned to him. There is but little certainty, but it is enough to show us the summit that his work reaches.

In this way we can start to become acquainted with *The Tempest*, as well as with his youthful work, the altar-piece of Castelfranco (Plates 8–9), with the *Concert Champêtre* and the *Sleeping Venus*, and we can study the deep humanity and the inexpressible charm of the landscape.

After Giorgione's early death his influence lived on in the heart-beat of art. And it needs intellectual courage to declare that in Giorgione's 12 lifetime the gigantic figure of Titian had not yet reached this height, although, in my opinion, he was the greatest of all Italian painters. As G. Fiocco stated, "As far as pictorial taste is concerned, Titian was the most congenial artist and yet, intellectually, he is far removed from Giorgione; Giorgione gave life to heaven and to dreams, Titian to earth, humanity and power."

These creations, with their unmistakable atmosphere, constitute a definite system of their own. For centuries there has been great uncertainty about their attribution. Experts waver between the pull of Giorgione and Titian. There is an equilibrium between the *Concert* in the Louvre and that in the Pitti; between the *Knight of Malta* and the *Gipsy Madonna* in Vienna, and the *Sacra Conversazione*, so marvellous in its tender tones (in the Prado). In R. Longhi's view it is utterly useless to try to tell Giorgione's effects from those of Titian in pictures painted just after 1510.

Whereas Giorgione's creative life was ephemeral and meteoric, Titian's was patriarchally long and unbelievably active, he lived to experience his third and even his fourth "youth".

Giorgione's life was mysterious and enigmatic, Titian's (1488/90–1576) dazzlingly rich and prolific. The long sequence of his hundreds of creations not only constitutes a gallery of masterpieces but, with its disguised or overt connections with real facts of life, with politics, with monarchs, and even with emperors and popes, provides us with a mass of historical evidence, from Charles V's victory at Mühlberg to the intricate vicissitudes that are revealed to us by the portraits of Pope Paul III and his nephews (Plate 15). While Giorgione's pictorial œuvre is intimate, elegiac and fanciful, delicately sensuous and musically lyrical, Titian's world is majestic, epic and transcendent and at the same time realistic, knightly and heroic.

Giorgione's world is the wonder of Venice; Titian's eye, on the other hand, was focused on the historical and human; his inquisitive and observing glance penetrates the most sumptuous and exalted courts of Europe: Rome and Augsburg, Austria, Spain, France, Ferrara, Mantua, Naples and Urbino.

Among all Giorgione's heirs Palma Vecchio (1480–1528) stands nearest to Titian. From the *Assumption of the Virgin* (1515–1518) in the Church of the Frari onwards, up to his death in 1528, Palma Vecchio, by using Giorgione's talent and evoking the burning shadow of Correggio, added something to Titian's already stupendous œuvre.

And to a lesser degree than the existing Giorgione–Titian problem, the Palma–Titian problem also awaits a solution. Although Palma, who was a native of Bergamo, whence he found his way to Venice, did not understand Titian's pictorial and moral strength, he felt his influence in art and in the use of light and colours. There are connections between Palma and Titian. Not only because Titian was able to retouch the pictures which Palma had left unfinished, but also because it is uncertain to which of the two artists some portraits are to be attributed, particularly the gloriously beautiful *Violante* in Vienna, which, in my view, is certainly Palma's work, though R. Longhi is convinced that it was painted by Titian.

Palma replaces the mysterious and exalted atmosphere of Giorgione's work by a serene and idyllic representation of nature. His pictures are permeated by a healthy humanism. Closest to Titian's work are the valuable details of his *Sacra Conversazione* or *Jacob's Encounter with Rachel* (in the Dresden Gallery).

From the second decade of the century onwards, that is to say from the time of Giorgione's death, Titian began to free himself from Giorgione's influence. In 1516–1518, the two years during which he painted the *Assumption of the Virgin* in the Church of the Frari, it became evident that he had even surpassed it. For two distinct forces were clearly at work simultaneously in the same spirit; take the *Sacra Conversazione* and the *Assumption of the Virgin*, both wholly New Testament in their inspiration, on the one hand, and the way in which *Sacred and Profane Love* is interpreted on the other. To display the fully clothed side by side with the nude is virtually poetry inspired by Lucretius and openly reveals a pagan and humanistic spirit. And since, at the same time, religious and profane thoughts had become intertwined, Titian created the *Bacchanalia* (Plate 12), *The Festival of Venus*, which is in the Prado, and *Bacchus and Ariadne*, which is preserved 14 in London. In one single grand ode these works sing the praises of life and nature. The three themes inspired by Philostratus, Catullus and Lucretius were realized in a healthy, Neo-Epicurean spirit. The Frari altar-piece, completed in 1526, is, of all Titians's art, the most solemn realization of architectural rhythm. Indeed, the master broke the tradition of compositional patterns, which had been introduced by Antonello, accepted by Giambellino and observed, though somewhat loosely, by Giorgione himself. Titian placed the scene diagonally, and shifted the compositional axis from the middle somewhat to the right. The Virgin is seated like a queen on a throne, within a framework of classical architecture, a design which only Veronese later adopted; he, too, preferred to set his compositions in magnificent architectural surroundings.

Vasari tells us that Titian met Michelangelo in Rome but was overwhelmed by his gigantic and awe-inspiring concepts. *The Magdalene, Christ Crowned with Thorns* (Louvre), or *St. John the Baptist* (in the Accademia in Venice) are works of this time (1535–1545), but the Roman master's influence can be discerned even more clearly in the clumsy canvases of the Church of the Salute in Venice.

But there was an exception when Titian's spirit, his independence and his authority did not give way: he created the marvellous figure of the *Venus of Urbino* about 1538 (Florence, Uffizi; Plates 13–14). It may be taken almost for certain that this figure depicts one of the mistresses, or perhaps the wife, of the Duke of Urbino. Together with this work others of his paintings, created at much the same time, extol the beauty of the female body; such, for example are the *Nude with Fur*, the *La Bella*. The figures resemble one another as if they were variations of the same face idealized in Titian's own way (the sitter is supposed to have been Eleonora Gonzaga).

This nude is often said to be the most beautiful Venus or nude woman Titian ever painted. The reminiscence of Giorgione's Venus (which bears traces of Titian's touch) is evident, though in the Venus of Urbino it is awakening and not sleep that is represented. The poetry of free natural scenery has been replaced by the human intimacy of a room; from the perspective of an infinite horizon gilded by the light of the setting sun,

15

we have entered the spatial restrictions of an interior, but an atmosphere that a Venetian brush interprets quite differently from, let us say, a Flemish one.

But before we reach the point where the crisis of Mannerism was overcome, and before we reach the marvellous phenomenon of self-renewal which took place between 1555 and 1558, we must examine a phase that was constant in Titian's work; and this is portrait-painting.

From Raphael to Velazquez, even to Van Dyck, no other master expressed so completely as Titian did public and private life, the external and the internal world. And yet there were times when portraiture was considered *genus humile et submissum*, an inferior form of art.

In the eloquent biography which this great master gives us of his historical heroes, people and facts come alive. A creative and sovereign impulse explores souls, penetrates characters, reveals secrets, and unflinchingly confronts imperial and royal crowns, tiaras and the power of monarchs. The characters march past and he, Titian, stops them for a moment and immortalizes them, vanquishing bodily frailty, human misery, sorrow, vanity and arrogance.

Many are those who march past us: Charles V, before and after the battle of Mühlberg, his son Philip II, with his soon-to-be-defeated "invincible" Armada, Francis I and Pope Paul, surrounded by his scheming nephews. The fine face of Isabel of Portugal, the ornament of Castile, shines before us; Gian Francesco d'Acquaviva, the insolent lancer, almost aflame in his red doublet, appears in a brilliant landscape and so does Francesco Maria della Rovere, the grandson of Pope Julius II, who was even more violent than his grandfather. The sea-green eyes of the man known sometimes as *Ippolito Riminaldi*, at others as *The Young Englishman*, radiate a mysterious attraction in the likeness in the Pitti Gallery; and the figure of the arrogant and shameless courtier Aretino is represented, a portrait of which the sitter himself once said: "It cannot be denied, it breathes, its pulse beats and it thinks just as I do in real life."

There is no doubt that Aretino was among the first to understand and praise the friend who, with extravagant generosity, called him "the *con-*

dottiere of literature... the glory of Italy." But the antagonism between the two men is proved by their portraits. Let us compare this portrait of Aretino with two likenesses of Titian. We are referring to the two self-portraits, one in Berlin, the other in the Prado, in which he appears in full possession of his powers. In the one he seems gentle and dignified, in the other, weary and suffering, immersed in thoughts.

Titian's last stylistic period began about 1558. According to Dell'Acqua "the master of Cadore (i.e. Titian) chose once again a serene pagan legend for his subject, and seemed thus to revert to the gay lyricism of his youthful work."

At that time the luminous *Danae* (Naples) was born, a work a variant of which, embellished with even more exciting light effects, is to be seen in the Prado. At that time he painted *Venus with the Organ-player* and the Venus entranced by her own beauty reflected by a mirror. One cupid holds the mirror, whilst another extends a garland to her.

Nevertheless, toward the end of the artist's life his horizon became darkened with the approach of suffering and death: *The Martyrdom of St. Lawrence* is a *nocturne* fraught with shadows. The scene, enclosed by a wall, is illuminated by the ghostly light of a smouldering fire. Such dramatic scenes are rare in Titian's art. The *Pietà*, unfinished on account of the artist's death, is like a Greek tragedy. Titian painted it *sibi et suis*, that is for himself and his family, for a family chapel which was to be built but which Fate snatched from him. His ashes rest in the Church of the Frari in Venice.

This *Pietà* strikes chords of Virgil; it is a pietà of man and God, a loud lament over Christ the man, blended with pity and sorrow for our own destiny. The tragic gesture Mary Magdalene makes is closely connected with the contemplation of death. Titian was unable to complete the picture, but Palma the Younger reverently finished it. His work in no way falsified or spoiled the marks of a genius which Titian displayed in his last work: the buoyancy of the texture, which, as it were, anticipated the technique of the Impressionists. In the light—which is like some sacrificial flame—the bodies virtually disintegrate, yet are restored by it to new

17

life. That is why Aretino wrote: "In Titian's... style there lives concealed the idea of a new nature."

For Heraclitus fire was the primary element of the world; for Titian it was colour. A whole generation followed this view, which exerted an effect on all the greatest painters of the period from Palma to Campagnola, from Veronese to Tintoretto and Bassano; it was on Titian's work that Van Dyck and Velazquez, Rubens, Rembrandt and Renoir fixed their gaze.

Titian's œuvre, the world he created, surpassed the limits of painting. His wonderful life would have been worthy of such biographers as Plutarch or Carlyle. In the catharsis of his art he rose above all ugliness, all evil and all tragedy. Himself purified he gazed on human misery and moral decline; he made peace between warring parties in civil strife, he succeeded in saving the radiant prestige of Venice and thus, in giving a new life, in the Venetian idiom, to the Italian phoenix.

His independence and distinct individuality assure an important place to the Veneto-Italian Lorenzo Lotto (*c.* 1480–1556), another of the century's outstanding masters and one who, too, was astonishingly prolific. His innate sense of colour made him a Venetian; his hues are vivid, at times almost aflame; they glitter like crystal in pure rose, sky-blue and rich red. He was so strong a personality that he did not submit passively to the influence of Giorgione or of Titian. Raphael touched him hardly at all and it seems as if he, also, intentionally ignored the world of Michelangelo's forms. Sebastiano del Piombo changed as a matter of course to the Roman, Michelangelesque style; Lotto, however, though he lived in Rome from 1509 to 1511, was unable to do so. In 1523 he moved to Bergamo, rediscovered the atmosphere of Venice, but also became exposed to new trends (from Leonardo to Bramante) and made the acquaintance of the, for him, exotic, tones of masters beyond the Alps. He had earlier studied Albrecht Dürer's œuvre and he later also discovered the other German and Swiss painters. To the very end he preserved his gentle and timid, soft melancholy and deeply humane personality, which comes to the fore in his best works, his profoundly revealing portraits. Sometimes he was

18

touched by mysticism, but he had nothing to do with the polemics and constraints of the Counter-Reformation. Possibly he did not even know about them.

He became separated from the ideas of his age; at times he even dialectically confronted them; his activity enriched the historical picture of the first half of the sixteenth century. Titian embodied the greatness and dignity of painting which formed its own history; in his representations of battle-scenes, allegories and victories, in his portraits of emperors, princes, popes and kings, he expressed, on the highest possible artistic level, the world of officialdom, fame and glory. Lotto's world, on the other hand, was rather that of the *petite-bourgeoisie*. His patrons were merchants, craftsmen and members of such families as the Martinengos and the Suardis, or other brilliantly-represented persons, who have survived with their suggestion of anonymity and with the enigmas of the symbols depicted in the portraits. Such are *Young Man with an Oil Wick* (Vienna, Kunsthistorisches Museum), *Portrait of a Nobleman* (Venice, Accademia; Plate 17). Titian's correspondence throws some light upon the connections he had with Augsburg and Rome, with Ferrara and Mantua, with Florence and Urbino and even with Madrid. Lotto's "account-book", which it has been possible to save from oblivion and destruction, tells us much about the painter's daily life.

Titian is laid bare in his correspondence; he took part in the history of his time and he was easily able to establish contacts with the outside world. Lotto's "account-book" is shrouded in the semi-darkness of moral consciousness, a consciousness nurtured by virtue and knowledge. Titian's correspondence helps us to write history itself; Lotto's "account-book" does no more than enable us faithfully to reconstruct his busy life and to understand the personality of a master whose existence is inseparably intertwined with the history of Veneto-Italian painting.

Strangely enough it was Aretino, who, from the moral point of view, is the least reliable among Lotto's contemporaries, who gave, just at that time, an opinion that was to hold its own even as a prophesy: "O, Lotto, thou art as kind as kindness itself, as virtuous as virtue itself..." Aretino

19

foresaw the "fame", that gradually attached itself to Lotto more than four centuries later. Lotto's contemporaries would not or could not acknowledge his greatness and only our own age has come to endow him with the appreciation which he deserves.

We have already mentioned Sebastiano del Piombo (*c.* 1485–1547), whose art was influenced by Giorgione's early works. A strange destiny shaped the work of Sebastiano Luciani, whose life can be divided into two clearly distinct phases. For centuries he has been known by two names; Sebastiano Viniziano unmistakably shows his origin; from 1531 onwards, however, when he was appointed "Keeper of the Lead" (*piombo* = lead), or Keeper of the Seal, in the Papal Chancellery in Rome, with that title's position and emoluments, he has been known as Sebastiano del Piombo (Plate 18).

R. Longhi considered him "the first artist to follow exclusively Giorgione's footsteps in his creations, ...on the wings of the organ doors of San Bartolomeo and even more in the altar-piece of San Giovanni Crisostomo". But later he became the most successful member of Michelangelo's very narrow circle of friends and on the basis of sketches by Michelangelo, he created the Pietà of Viterbo and of Ubeda. The two phases of the artist's life are completely separate. Up to the beginning of 1511 he was typical of the most consistent Veneto style: he created works that suited Giorgione's world and that radiated Giorgione's atmosphere; Sebastiano had drawn on Giorgione's spirituality for pictorial virtues and qualities. He was well-versed in music, too. According to tradition both Piombo and Giorgione were excellent lute-players.

Brescia, after the tragic vicissitudes of Scaligeri, Visconti and Malatesta rule, became part of the Serenissima, that is to say, of the Republic of Venice, in 1426. From the standpoint of painting, Brescia remained Lombard in the Quattrocento; its greatest master and innovator was Vincenzo Foppa (1427/30–1515/16). In the sixteenth century the town played an outstanding role in Venetian painting. The 150 years from the mid-fifteenth century to the end of the sixteenth were the golden age of grand painting, renewed in the Venetian meaning of the term. Indeed Brescia became a part of the Venetian school, with such members as Savoldo and Romanino, Moretto and Moroni.

It was to the now "Venetianizer" Brescia that young Caravaggio himself went to study "Realism".

The first member of the group of four was Girolamo Savoldo, a contemporary of Lotto (*c.* 1480–1548 or later), not only in time, but also in respect of his creative powers.

The altar-piece that he made in Pesaro, which is now to be seen in the Brera, shows him to have been as powerful an artist as Titian is proved to have been by his *Assumption of the Virgin* in the Church of the Frari. Savoldo's Christmas pictures in Turin and Brescia reveal an intimate, bucolic mood; while his portraiture is markedly vigorous (as is evinced by the so-called Gaston de Foix portrait).

Whether we examine his youthful experiments in Florence or his mature period in the Veneto, he shows himself in all his work to have been a humane and individual painter; with his hermits, his shepherds and his flute-players he is an intimate poet of nature (Plate 19). Critics have acknowledged that Savoldo was the forerunner of the great Flemish and Spanish masters.

Girolamo di Romano (1484/87–1562), known as Romanino, who began as a definite member of the Lombard school (Civerchio, Foppa), was later to join with enthusiasm the artists of the Veneto, indeed of Venice itself and he entered the world of Giorgione. He also became acquainted with him through Titian's and Pordenone's paintings.

The frescoes of the cathedral in Cremona and of the Castle of Malpaga near Bergamo are important works of his; the two cycles bear witness to the artist's explosive narrative talents. Mention should also be made of his portraits, which fascinate with their lavish pomp, and are preserved in Bergamo and in Budapest (Plate 20).

Alessandro Bonvicino, known as Moretto (*c.* 1498–1554) evinces in his works the teaching of Romanino and Savoldo, but his vigorous qualities as a painter testify to the invincible and lively effect of Venetian painting. He transformed even the elements of Mannerism and the influence of

21

Raphael so much that they became muted in the eloquence of the Venetian tradition. He succeeded in establishing a homogeneous and unique artistic individuality, which embraced differing manifestations; one of these is Romantic (for example, Justina and the humbly-kneeling donor with the unicorn in a luminous, lyrical landscape, Vienna); the other is serenely classical (in this style the artist was able to create solemn altar-pieces with sculpturesque figures, such as the *Assumption of the Virgin* (*c.* 1525), in the old Cathedral of Brescia, and finally, the simple, humane and utterly realistic approach of the portraitist, who observes and depicts the sitter with perfect effectiveness. With this activity he opened up the way to Moroni (Plate 21). The love of colourism led him to a complete identification with the Venetians' palette; indeed, to create St. Ursula he borrowed the scheme from Vivarini.

While his complex approach contained noble and courtly features, he was also the powerful initiator of Lombard "Realism", and thus, in the company of saints, knights and their ladies "there appear the first beggarly and naked prophets, together with the first evangelists sitting cross-legged ... and even one or two bourgeois saints, who look more like card-players painted by Caravaggio" (R. Longhi).

One of the first significant representatives of the Brescia school, a school which strove to express Realism was Giovanni Battista Moroni (Bergamo, 1520/1530?–1578). His early mood of painting narrative and pious pictures dried up, but he underwent a new birth and achieved fame as a portrait-painter. In this genre—in which he records the human spirit—he penetrated below the surface and became a master, not only because of his individual style and his skill, but also because he professed the inspiring freedom of art and stood up against the rules dictated by the Counter-Reformation, against censorship and restrictions. Together with this realistic use of portraiture the fashion of depicting still-life also gained ground. It began in Cremona, reached Milan by way of the young Caravaggio, and then it spread throughout Italy and even affected Venice, though there it aroused less interest.

Moroni was so skilful in portraying people that one of his portraits   **22** was ascribed to Titian, who is said to have urged the Venetian governors stationed in Bergamo to sit for Moroni, because his portraits were so faithful to nature (Plate 22).

Moroni was a sober, persevering observer, always aiming at the essential. His profound penetration enables him to represent faces and customs; he was rational, too, in his emotions. He could easily adjust himself to his bourgeois surroundings and meet its demands. He was a worthy and historically accurate chronicler of his world; but even in his most life-like portraits he preserved lyrical qualities, such as are to be found, for example, in the *Portrait of a Sculptor* (Vienna), which supposedly represents Alessandro Vittoria.

In April, 1559, Henry II of France and Philip II of Spain signed the treaty of Cateau-Cambrésis. Italy was now vassal of Spain and only Venice was able to save some of its dignity and freedom, that Venice which, in the words of Tommaso Moncenigo, "...is the only state, ...the only part... the only corner of Italy that is still free", that Venice, which had been hailed by Aretino as early as in 1530 as "Universal Motherland! Free land of all! Home of the homeless!."

Political and artistic values well illustrate Venice's historic position. Politically it is enough to remember the firmness with which the Republic rejected the endeavours of the Papacy to interfere in its internal affairs.

Not much heed was paid in Venice to the "Index" or to the resolutions of the Council of Trent concerning questions of art. We may well see cause and effect in the matter of the rights of freedom which the Republic ensured and the creative power, buoyancy and imagination of its artists. Painters indeed turned the Venetian Cinquecento into the golden age of painting; the second half of the century was worthy in every way of the first fifty years.

When the Mannerist crisis—which, indeed, had touched everybody—had been mastered, a new generation appeared, with the aim of "renewing Venetian art". This new generation had only one member who created something new with miraculous spontaneity and animation—and that was

Titian. In the last twenty years of his life he marched, more than ever before, in the vanguard of the moderns. All the other masters who had been adherents of Mannerism had died well before 1560; Lotto, for example, died as a lay brother in Loreto in 1556.

It was in this atmosphere that Jacopo Robusti, called Tintoretto (1518–1594), grew up. He could not wholly escape the effect of Mannerist tastes, but with his exceptionally strong personality he overcame them, and later he turned against them. Instead of temperance and restraint he chose intemperance and exuberance. He confronted schools and academies with his own tempestuous impulsiveness; for the Tuscan-Roman *delineavit* (sketched, outlined) he substituted the *pinxit* (painted) of the Venetians, in spite of the fact that among the Venetians it was he for whom drawing was the most important. He is characterized by constant and sudden passionate impulses. He was a born painter, a mere stroke of his brush was vigorous and full of life. Passing over his complicated years of study, we should like merely to note that the spectacular start of his career can be dated from his picture *St. Mark Rescuing a Slave*, probably painted in 1548 (Venice, Accademia; Plate 23). This, with its vivid animation and its dazzling light, was indeed a startling and revolutionary work. This picture and *The Last Supper* (Plate 26) in the San Giorgio Maggiore determined Tintoretto's œuvre for forty-six years, right to the end of his amazingly rich career. In the picture of *The Last Supper* composed diagonally, light illuminates the interior with a dramatic force reminiscent of Rembrandt; the sulphurous glimmer of the hanging lamp is drowned by a dazzling halo, that of Christ, who has broken the bread and is giving it to the Apostles.

Not for a moment did Tintoretto's impetus flag during this long period—almost half a century—and thus his work was fast and his brushwork passionate. Vasari, who was at a loss when facing this manner of painting, wrote: "Sometimes he refurbished, with hard work, sketches that he had left unfinished, to show that he painted haphazard and out of pride rather than because of the drawing or because he had a carefully thought-out plan." "He spends less time on painting than on finding out what he should paint."

24

Dramatic qualities, force and dynamism are characteristic of all Tintoretto's works. His dramatic power—like that of Michelangelo—often becomes awe-inspiring. His faith is independent of rules, and worships man as the protagonist of a world where happiness is born of pain and comes to new life from martyrdom and death.

Tintoretto created two Pantheons of his own: in the Scuola di San Rocco and in the Madonna dell'Orto, where he wanted to be buried. It is impossible to sum up or survey his œuvre successfully if we leave out of consideration the works created in these two places, for in them every conceivable thought and style can be found.

A characteristic example of Tintoretto's pictorial approach is the *Ariadne, Venus and Bacchus* (Plates 24–25) in the Doges' Palace, this paean of mythological love. It was also here, in the Palace, that he created his enormous *Paradise*, and it was he who was commissioned to create a solemn hymn to the glory of Venice in the magnificent suite of the Doge.

It is by no means due to pure chance that, some years before his death, Paolo Veronese painted *The Apotheosis of Venice* (Plate 30) on an oval canvas in the same room, the Hall of the Great Council—the room which Jacopo Tintoretto had glorified with his own eternal *Paradise*.

Paolo Veronese (1528–1588) started work in the workshop of his father, a stone-carver. He probably followed his father's trade while a boy and then became a pupil of Antonio Badile, who was his senior by only ten years. He married the daughter of his master, and it was his wife who first inspired the type of women he painted. Andrea Mantegna's art had a decisive effect on the shaping of his personality, though he was even more deeply influenced by Classic and Neo-Classic architecture, the latter chiefly through Palladio.

He may have obtained the idea of pictorial decoration from the ceiling of the Camera degli Sposi in Mantua, a work by Mantegna, it may have been here that Veronese saw a perfect harmony between architectural lines and figures.

We know but few of Veronese's youthful works. His rise was stupendous; at the age of twenty-five (1553) he was already in Venice, where he settled and worked from 1558 to 1560 in the Doges' Palace and in the Church of St. Sebastian.

The Villa Barbaro at Maser (Treviso), a world-famous and precious example of the Renaissance villa, has been saved from the ravages of war. In it the art of Palladio and Veronese conjures up the ancient, noble morals of Italy; it evokes Horace and Catullus and even the Medicis and Caterina Cornaro.

Though the painter was scarcely 32 years old when he was at Maser, everything there foretold his future. Here we can admire the serenity and seriousness that suits things considered sacred, all Olympus for instance. In these works, in landscapes and in tales of mythology, he sings the praises of life. He examines everything with shy rapture and he is permeated with a humanity which is at once simple and traditional, spiritual and sensuous. The flame of the senses is muted in these tenderly glowing nudes; silks, brocades and damasks decorate the majestic nakedness of gods and virtues. The subtle range of colours from scarlet to various shades of green and the fabulous turquoise—a tint which for centuries has borne his, Veronese's, name—is fascinating. His cool, silvery white or ivory colours are blended or veiled with the brilliance of mother-of-pearl.

The so-called Last Suppers can also be considered hymns to life. Though they pretend to represent New Testament scenes, they are actually profane feasts and banquets.

Perhaps the oldest among these holy or profane representations is the *Supper in the Pharisee's House*. The composition is the simplest possible: the architectural elements are used schematically, as if they were stage sets.

About 1560 he may have painted the first variant of *The Wedding Feast at Cana*, which is preserved in Dresden, whereas the one in the Louvre may be dated at 1562. This latter picture, which is larger in size, is of a more intricate composition than previous ones of the same theme, or than the *Last Supper* in the Accademia in Venice. The overall picture is more animated and restless, and the approach is more stagy and choreographic. The "small concert" in the centre of the picture contains the musical element, it is the focal point of the composition and completes the ideology of these 26 worthy hedonists; it is a witness, too, to the co-existence of the arts and to the fact that they were essential parts of Venetian life.

Let us look at *The Feast at the House of Levi* (Plates 27–28; Venice, Accademia), which virtually expands the atmosphere with its gaiety and rises to the highest power of expression. The scene of the feast has hardly been changed; it reflects as always the artist's picture of the world, his hedonistic, Neo-Pagan view of life; in this instance the dithyrambic hymn happens to represent a feast.

In Veronese's paintings of the Last Supper, Christ, the Apostles, the Virgin, Mary Magdalene, Gregory and others sit at table with a natural simplicity. All secrets, all miracles have vanished; no longer does the praying human being humiliate himself when offering his votive gift. The traditional Italian methods of vine-growing are revived in the wine at Cana, the poetry and music of Athens, Rome and humanism come to new life in the "Feast". The composition is a hymn to life by an artist who is a Neo-Epicurean but who also knows the Gospel very well.

From its narrow-minded, bigoted and reactionary point of view the Counter-Reformation interpreted the picture quite correctly: it accused Veronese of heresy and launched a prosecution against him. The artist's reply was almost a minor treatise on aesthetics: in it he demanded the absolute moral independence of art. Indeed, the sovereignty of the Republic and the power of its laws saved the work from the effects of censorship and ensured the civil rights of the Venetian citizen Paolo Caliari (Veronese).

The same spirit of independence imbues Veronese's picture *The Rape of Europa* (Plate 29), which was created not much later, between 1576 and 1580, "for the inspection of Signor Jacopo Contarini". In 1713 Bertucci Contarini bequeathed the work to the Republic and it was hung in the hall of the Anticollegio, beside Jacopo Tintoretto's mythological composition *Ariadne, Venus and Bacchus*. Perhaps it is its poetic qualities that make this picture Veronese's *chef-d'œuvre*, quite apart from the historical fact that from being a Venetian work it became a truly European creation. Its artistic importance is not only that it lives in so many different variants and that it gave inspiration to so great a number of artists; but also that it

27

opened up the way to the most delicate Rococo and provided precious encouragement even to Watteau and Boucher.

The artist no longer sought the company of those in power; he seems to avoid princes, popes and tyrants, and made no attempt to gain their favour. But he was accorded appreciation both by Venice and by his fellow-artists. He was a quiet man, indifferent to ephemeral matters, and leathing the commonplace. He avoided company and lived a solitary life in his art. He was reticent and tactfully silent. There were no adventures or external complications in his life; only once was he forced into the "lawsuit" of the Inquisition. His features bear witness to his modesty and pride alike.

He was a portraitist of the bourgeoisie and he also painted group-pictures, for example one of the Cuccina family (Dresden), but he "never strove to obtain any employment", that is to say, he did not humiliate himself to obtain commissions.

However, there is a wonderful painting of his, in which peasants and shepherds, simple people, that is to say, are depicted; it is *The Adoration of the Shepherds* in the Church of SS. Giovanni e Paolo in Venice. Clearly this work pointed to a new course in Venetian painting, which was to be pursued by Jacopo Bassano and his family.

What we know about the artist Jacopo da Ponte, called Bassano (*c.* 1515–1592) we owe, first of all, to modern research, for in the three centuries following his death he was first misunderstood and then neglected.

While a peasant youth in Bassano, he saw Lotto and Titian in Venice. Soon he painted his first works: variants of *The Assumption of the Virgin* in the altar-piece at Asolo, and putti and angels in Titian's style. In the middle of the century he was deeply influenced by the many different trends of Venetian painting. At the same time he too exerted an effect on Venetian painters, even on Tintoretto himself.

However, Bassano's personality was really liberated only when he returned home. Once again in the country, he elaborated the impressions he had gained; in his imagination he transformed them and created his own world and with it his individual and inimitable style (Plate 31). Later, **28** rather dull imitations of decadent successors produced a narrative genre with peasants and popular figures; this, however, was far below the master's talents and even his intentions. Thus Jacopo Bassano initiated a certain trend of "genre-painting", though he was not responsible for its low artistic level. Markets, caravans, household utensils, trades, beasts of burden and barnyard fowl, the spoils of the chase, patriarchal families or gipsies became the objects of scenes depicted by Bassano. This whole world was brilliantly represented in a style in which he used vigorous, gay spots of colour. This style made Boschini declare that this "endoved light" was manifested

in the spots, in the brush-strokes that
are like precious stones:
fire-red, emerald, turquoise pearls,
diamonds ablaze in the dark night.

But it should not be forgotten that this "nature poetry" was in no way related to folklore; it was as noble and classic as Tasso's *Aminta* (1573) or Guarini's *Faithful Shepherd* (1590); though it was pastoral in its character, it was by no means decadent in the manner of Arcadia, nor was it formulated in a narrow vernacular.

Bolognese artists and the Carraccis follow Cinquecento Venetian painting; today its effect on French painters of the seventeenth, eighteenth and nineteenth centuries is well-known, from Poussin—who made copies of the putti of Titian's Bacchanals—to Delacroix.

And thus we have reached the Seicento, a century which means disparage and loathe, but which others praise and appreciate anew; we have reached the period which the history of art calls Baroque.

Caravaggio's painting did not exert an effect on Venetian painting of the late sixteenth century, although the artist visited the city in order to see Venetian painters face to face. At this time of decline Venice discovered that her influence was bearing fruit everywhere except in the city of lagoons itself. Alienated from new trends which it had itself created, Venetian painting virtually became its own prison.

Yet Venice continued to play the role of a Mæcenas, and thus offered a new impetus to her artists' work. State commissions for the Doges' Palace and commissions of public and private institutions and of the patricians maintained the pictorial traditions of Venice, although parasites squandered much of the magnificent heritage.

The arrival, and then the prolific work, of three foreign masters, the Roman Fetti, the German Liss and the Genoese Strozzi lent a new impetus to Seicento Venetian painting. But this spiritual and formal renewal could not have materialized without the almost magic strength and mysterious regenerative power of Venice and her painting, which were based on traditions and living aesthetic surroundings and were fed on the enchanting natural beauty of the nature of the world of the lagoons.

The young Roman painter Domenico Fetti (1589–1624) was the first of the three to arrive in Venice. He had already become acquainted, in Mantua, with the works of Mantegna, Titian and Tintoretto and he began to realize what "being a Venetian" meant. In 1621 he went to Venice and lived there till his death at the age of 35 (Plate 32). He evoked Elsheimer's landscapes, allied himself with Bassano's efforts and produced precious small paintings. He was fondest of "Georgic scenes expressed in the form of parables" (Fiocco). His best creations are preserved in Vienna, Kassel and Dresden *(Workers in a Vineyard, The Blind, The Morra-Game, The Lost Drachma)*.

The German Jan Liss (*c.* 1595–1629) pursued a similar, though more complicated, course before he reached Venetian painting. He was born in Oldenburg at the end of the sixteenth century. He lived in Holland and arrived in Venice about 1620; he left for Rome, where he became acquainted with Caravaggio's works, but returned to Venice in 1623 to settle down there for good and it was there that he died. For over a year he often met Fetti and became his faithful follower, so much so that Fetti's *David* was considered to be Liss's work. He fell in love with Tintoretto's artistic fervour and with Paolo Veronese's sensuous tenderness. He adopted cer-

30

tain tentative Baroque features of Rubens's art and began to feel the charm of Rococo. He worked with lively imagination and with exuberant and animated vigour. He was first and foremost interested in the events of everyday life, many of whose picturesque episodes he recorded. But he did not disdain popular backgrounds. He painted vulgar themes—for instance brothels—with a keen and witty eye; he interpreted brilliantly the morra-game (Kassel, Gallery), fighting peasants (Nuremberg, Museum) and he realized all this with fluid, delicate brushwork and masterly elegance. A characteristic example of these qualities is his *Venus in front of the Mirror* (Florence, Uffizi; Plate 33). The way in which the German master approached the Settecento Rococo, which hovered between Piazzetta and Tiepolo, is indeed astonishing.

Through the mediation of Fetti, some of whose creations he even copied, Liss deliberately transformed his art into Venetian; whereas the Genoese Bernardo Strozzi (1581–1644) followed the example and guidance of both in developing into a Venetian, perhaps indeed under the direct influence of Liss's œuvre. He was a mature painter when he left Genoa and arrived in Venice in 1630, at the age of 49. He may have wanted to escape the discomforts of monastic life, or even perhaps, arrest. Under the influence of the Ligurian-Tuscan painter Sorri and of art beyond the Alps, Strozzi's artistic personality had firmly developed in his native town. *The Tribute Money* (several copies and a variant by his own hand—to be found in Budapest—are known), the *Madonna* (in the Querini Stampalia Palace), *The Annunciation* (Budapest) and *Rebecca and Eleazar* (Dresden), were produced in his first Venetian period. Chance or good luck enable us to compare Liss and Strozzi with each other, since *The Charity of St. Lawrence* (Plate 34) is in the Church of San Niccolò da Tolentino in Venice and opposite it there is Liss's work *The Ecstasy of St. Jerome*. Strozzi's work is characterized by glowing colours, by free and well-modelled brushwork and by sober, calm naturalism.

Of the three painters from abroad, it was Strozzi who exerted the greatest influence; it was an influence that few painters could escape. However, from the point of view of the development of art certain minor

31

masters in the Veronese tradition were more important: Antonio Molinari (1665–1727) and Gregorio Lazzarini (1657–1735), through whose art, in the hands of their pupils Piazzetta and Tiepolo, Settecento painting came into being.

However, before discussing the eighteenth century, this glorious final chord of Venetian painting, we must briefly refer to the historic circumstances which led relentlessly from the drama of Cambrai to the tragedy of the Peloponnesus, and to the signing of the "Napoleonic Peace Treaty" of Campoformio (17th October 1797), which, at the same time, meant the end of the glorious Republic.

Vasco da Gama's venture had dealt a heavy blow to the economic life and commerce of Venice. By sailing round the Cape of Good Hope, at the southern tip of Africa, the Portuguese sailor opened up a new route to India, and left to Venice the longer, uncomfortable and dangerous land route (1497). More and more merchants left the Rialto. The Venetians' endeavours—which were a signpost to the future—to reach the East from the Mediterranean by means of an artificial waterway, also failed. Evidence of this is to be seen in the Louvre even today. One of Bellini's followers represented the arrival of the Doge Domenico Trevisani in Cairo, to discuss the building of a canal. (Only more than three centuries later did the plan materialize.)

But then good luck did not desert the Republic for good, for it was only a short time afterwards that the Venetians scored a glorious victory at Lepanto (October, 1571), which was followed by the twenty-five-year Cretan War, with the occupation of the Dardanelles as its highest achievement. It was on the 17th July 1657 that the brilliant general Lazzaro Mocenigo lost his life on board his ship in the same way as had Lorenzo Marcello a year before in the same Straits. But these glorious episodes were in vain: the Republic, the Serenissima, lost the war in 1669. And although later, in the last war fought by the Venetian navy, Admiral Morosini was the winner finally, in the peace treaty of Passarovich in 1718, Venice lost the Peloponnesus, Crete and the island of Tenos.

The last of the great Venetian admirals, Angelo Emo, carried out only police actions against the pirates of Tripoli, Tunisia and Algeria between 1766 and 1777. The German Archenholz stated in 1788 that in no other European state were signs of so profound a decline discernible as in Venice. Goethe had noticed the same two years before.

In this grave economic and political situation, the dire selfishness of the ruling oligarchy turned a deaf ear to all new ideas. It grew more and more reactionary, and cruelly persecuted every new thought, as well as any people or groups professing them.

In vain had the Bastille been destroyed, in vain did the French Revolution achieve victory in 1793: Venice, which Aretino had called a citadel of freedom, became the last resort of conservative reaction.

And yet it was not only adventurers and cardsharpers who poured into Venice; some of the greatest men of the age, too, flocked to the city. They did not want to see a dying, declining Venice, but a city still alive in her history. Let us recall only Goethe, Brosses, Montesquieu and Rousseau, or among the literary figures of Italy, Maffei and Metastasio; or young Foscolo, who wished to see the ravages of Venice only in order to write his indignation at what he saw. Byron arrived, with his *Weltschmerz*, Schopenhauer came and Ruskin, and Browning and Wagner came to die here.

In printing houses and libraries the pomp of the Aldinis rose to new life: Gaspare Gozzi, with his famous *Osservatore*, can be considered the father of journalism.

Many famous theatres were playing in the city: it was here that the historic process took place in the course of which *commedia dell'arte* became an animated comedy of characters played in costumes, a comedy in which the actors did not wear masks. It was here that Pietro Chiari's and Carlo Gozzi's prolific literary work—as opposed to Goldoni's—was displayed.

Starting from, and imitating, scenes of the straight theatre, the musical theatre emerged, and this brought about an amazing development of music. As early as the seventeenth century Venice had outstanding composers: Andrea and Giovanni Gabrieli, and it had Monteverdi, always "the most modern", the creator of "music drama". In the Settecento music came to be further enriched by such masters as Marcello, Galuppi of Burano, and Vivaldi, the greatest of them all, who composed his works under the magic spell of nature.

Diplomacy also came to life again and tried to save the honour and fame of Venice, the city which Lionello Venturi described as "the most brilliant and, at the same time, the most glorious centre of painting, not only in Italy, but in the whole of Europe, too . . .". "It was first of all through Venice that the Settecento became great."

The Venetian ambassador to Spain, Giovanni Querini, tried to use Tiepolo's stay in Madrid to conclude a treaty with the King of Spain more favourable for the Serenissima. A number of Venetian painters were living abroad: Canal in London, Bellotto (Canaletto) in Dresden, Vienna, Turin and Warsaw, Crosato in Piedmont, Fontebasso in Petersburg, Pellegrini in the Netherlands, Paris and London, Amigoni in Germany, Rosalba Carriera in Paris, Vienna and Modena and her brother-in-law G. A. Pellegrini in England, Germany, the Low Countries, Paris and Vienna.

While Venetian painting had reached the last period of its golden age, in Germany a new movement, which was to become its very antithesis, was emerging. The role of colour was questioned and it was declared to be an element of "poisonous effect", alien to aesthetical experiences; in the same way as any heterogeneous element would contaminate water, so—it was maintained—colours rendered art "impure" and imbued it with a sinful sensuousness. Sculpture came to be extolled and there was a return to the painting of sterile and colourless *grisailles*, which imitated the sculptures of Antiquity.

Neo-Classicist theories adopted once again the Greek ideal of beauty, although Winckelmann, the theoretician of the new trend, had never seen original creations of Greek sculpture. This theory sought and upheld non-existent interactions, connections and inheritances from a distant past of his own making; Venetian painting, on the other hand, had preserved in its historic and artistic reality the variety of its forms, the lavishness of colours and, as a symbol of Italian painting, has remained an eternally 34 living, inalienable part of European culture. The apostle of Winckelmann's theory was Raphael Mengs, and his greatest victim was Canova. At once opponents sprung up in Venice: G. B. Piranesi and G. B. Tiepolo, although Canova himself was also a native of the Veneto. Mengs, the miserable courtier of Augustus III in Dresden, arrived in Spain in 1761, only a few months before Tiepolo's arrival. In Madrid Mengs, who was considered to be "the reformer of the perverted painting of the Baroque and Rococo", attacked one definite target: Tiepolo in person and his paintings in the Palace. Winckelmann brought discredit upon himself in the opinion of posterity when he declared: "To see Tiepolo and to forget him is the matter of a moment, whereas Mengs remains immortal." Mengs continued struggling in Rome and Italy and did not realize that even in his own lifetime he was losing touch with the currents of his time. Gian Battista Piranesi, who could pride himself on having the best taste in Rococo art, survived Winckelmann by ten years and became the forerunner of the vigorous and passionate trend that was given the name Romanticism; he can at least be considered as a Pre-Romantic. Piranesi like Canova, was also born in the Veneto, his native village was Magliano Veneto.

Mengs's arrogance was of no avail; Venetian painting, whose inspiring influence made itself felt all through the eighteenth century, adhered to its own glorious past and to its best traditions.

Through their pupils and their œuvre some seventeenth-century painters opened up the way to the Settecento. But the two Riccis, Sebastiano and Marco, played not merely the role of intermediaries; they were individuals, both of them.

We cannot follow the years of Sebastiano Ricci's (c. 1659–1734) schooling. He had travelled far before he reached Venice. He had been not only to Bologna, Parma, Piacenza, Rome and Florence but to Paris and London as well. When he returned to the Veneto he was virtually reborn. Venice freed him from all restraints and from the effects of many different cultures, and gave him back his Venetian character. His last creation The Assumption of the Virgin (Vienna, Karlskirche) is a fine composition, bright with colour.

A lively sketch of this work, displaying a veritable bravura of brushwork, is preserved in the Budapest Museum of Fine Arts (Plate 35).

In the course of an adventurous life his nephew Marco Ricci (1676–1729) had gained experiences which matured his singular personality. Thanks to him, the trend, inaccurately termed "minor masters' painting", was separated from the current of ordinary "genres"; it was both liberated and raised to a high artistic rank. Sketch-like landscapes with ruins were given new life, new emotions and poetic rhythm. These lyrical qualities of landscape painting demand nimble brushwork and a freely soaring fantasy (Plate 36). His drawings, too, are of exceptional value. Nearly all of them are pen-drawings and reveal great vigour even when Marco Ricci transcribed other masters' drawings (those he made of Titian's are outstanding). They are, of course, no less vigorous when he adhered more faithfully to the reality of nature. Collections of his drawings are preserved in Vienna, London and Windsor. The canvas *Ruins with Figures* in the museum of Vicenza is an excellent example of Sebastiano's and Marco's collaboration. The Venetian character of Marco's œuvre must be especially emphasized. His style lived on till Zuccarelli and Zais and his effect can be well discerned in the work of Francesco Guardi.

Owing to his different origin, personality and culture Giovanni Battista Piazzetta (1682–1754) was antagonistic to the Ricci trend. A parallel can be drawn between his school and that of Tiepolo.

Piazzetta had inherited his artistic vein from his father, a simple wood-carver. It was Molinari who led him to painting and this guidance was significant from the very beginning, because it directed him towards "naturalistic" art in the meaning which this term had in the Veneto, and introduced him to the best works of Liss and Strozzi. Piazzetta achieved his effects by a powerful contrast of light and dark areas, and by rendering the feel of the things he depicted in a graphically realistic manner. But in his innovations he relied essentially on two sources only: the art of Crespi, the Bolognese, and Solimena, the Neapolitan. He visited Crespi and lived with him as his pupil; but it was only a spiritual link, a distant affinity, that connected him with Solimena.

In some of his memorable pictures Piazzetta captures the floating of bodies in air, the state between levitation and ecstasy. Such are the *Immaculate Conception* in Parma, *The Ecstasy of St. Francis* in Vicenza, but, above all, the ceiling-painting in the Church of SS. Giovanni e Paolo in Venice which represents *St. Dominic in Glory*. It was the first time that the vaults of infinity had opened up in Venice and that rising bodies had swirled with such tempestuous force. There are almost no lines in this composition, just colours dazzling in the sunshine.

But Piazzetta painted not only altar-pieces and religious pictures; he also observed everyday life with liking and interest. A seduction scene is depicted in his picture of Rebecca at the well (Milan, Brera)—in this excellent genre-painting a rope of pearls is being offered to a charming, blonde girl,—he shows a *Fortune-Teller*, who tells the future from the lines of the palm; this charming scene evokes the atmosphere of the best French works of the eighteenth century (Venice, Accademia; Plate 37); sometimes he created veritable gems of narrative art by representing for instance intimate scenes of home life, with the figure of the cook or the housemaid.

His school reacted intensely to his art. Bencovich stands first among his followers; to such an extent that the works of the master often cannot be told from those of the pupil. As already mentioned, Piazzetta influenced young Tiepolo, too.

Although his school popularized the master's art, and thus temporarily brought about his triumph, it also contributed to its decline, for the mediocrity of his followers dimmed the light of his art. The polemics of Neo-Classicism, which soon flared up, also played a part in causing Piazzetta's name to be forgotten. Tiepolo had at least the honour of becoming Winckelmann's and Mengs's target in the course of this argument. Piazzetta—who, according to Pallucchini, could be called "the Courbet of the Venetian Settecento"—was soon forgotten; to have been elected first president of the Accademia di Belle Arti in Venice cannot have been more than a hollow consolation, by a decree of the Republic dated 24th September 1750 for the master, who died four years later.

37   The father of Giovanni Battista Tiepolo (1696–1770), the most charac-

teristically Venetian painter of the eighteenth century, was a seafaring man, who died in 1697, leaving his little son, then one year old, to Orsetta, the boy's mother. Of her we only know that she had an ancient Venetian name and that she was the first to recognize her son's genius. She did all she could to advance his artistic development.

Tiepolo's genius unfolded early. He studied the glorious course of Venetian painting from the eighth to the fifteenth century, and drew modestly upon its sources. With his excellent sense of colour, composition and form, he was able to reveal endless space, the whole world. Although he possessed some of Titian's calm, supreme power, and some of Tintoretto's dramatic swing and eternal *fortissimo*, his most evident kinship was with Veronese. Indeed, it was with almost Dantesque inevitability that the two masters should meet as Venetians. It was with an identical spiritual approach that they guessed the mystery of creation and of life, and both were able to interpret it pictorially.

Tiepolo's blossoming and sensuous humanism was sometimes combined with subtle sadness.

The heritage of the Renaissance, still unaffected by Rationalism and Enlightenment, came to new life in Tiepolo's works in the eighteenth century. The master was faithful to Ariosto's fanciful images of chivalry, but also to the Classic and Roman interpretation of myths and of the Gospels. As a result of this, Veronese's painting *The Feast at the House of Levi* and Tiepolo's *The Feast of Cleopatra* (Stockholm, National Museum, and London, Alexander Collection) are depicted identically not only because of similar pictorial tastes; the spiritual motif of *agape* itself is an organic part of their aspect of life and finds expression again after a gap of two centuries in an idiom almost identical with the earlier one. The differences between the two are the inevitable results of the passing of time. In fact Tiepolo was a Renaissance personality.

From 1715, the first date on record up to 1770, the date of his death in Madrid, 55 years of his life were spent in creative work, work which can be critically inspected. During this time an œuvre of gigantic dimensions came into being—an œuvre that embarrasses by its quantity and amazes by its quality, since Tiepolo created relatively few works that could not stand the test of time.

This œuvre is a grand symphonic *ensemble* serving the great cosmic problem of life and is made up of sacred and profane tales of different ages. His most suitable, indeed his inborn medium is the fresco, the most classic, eternal, strongest and most architectonic way of expression in terms of murals. The artist imagined his work in the forms of frescoes; there is, as it were, nothing premeditated in them, as though he were improvising all the time. His frescoes are never empty interpretations of his sketches, they are always surprising, magical, spontaneous and rich in colours and chromatic variations. They are pictorial, lyrical ecstasies; they are like sonnets, terse and self-contained.

Tiepolo transferred the whole of life into a heavenly setting, a setting which enchants the spectator and softens even the cruel scenes that were popular in the Seicento, such as, for instance, the sacrifice of Isaac or Iphigenia. The brilliant colours, the gorgeous buildings, costumes and fabrics, the vault of heaven all tame the plot and deprive it of its sanguinary nature; in this way a biblical story or a mythological scene becomes natural and serene. In the mural of the Villa Valmarana in Vicenza the pictorial lyricism of the master even enriches all the variants of the ancient theme of Iphigenia which Euripides, Racine and Goethe formulated in words and Scarlatti, Gluck, and Jommelli in music.

Tiepolo worked in the Villa Valmarana in Berico with the same vigour and intention as did Veronese in the Maser Villa of the Barbaro family. The classic mythology of the *Aeneid* and of the *Iliad* alternates here with the tales of chivalry, with the sylvan poetry of Arcadia, with Angelica and Medoro among the shepherds; in Tiepolo's art we are confronted with a freely soaring, late interpretation of Homer, Virgil, Tasso and Ariosto.

Tiepolo loved country life and had a cottage built at Zianigo, but fate did not allow him to enjoy it. However, his son Gian Domenico revealed to us a new world with the frescoes he painted there: this world is populated by clowns, hunchbacks, jesters and satyrs.

39   The father would often paint monumental historic frescoes glorifying

an entire family: in Venice he paid tribute to the Rezzonicos and the Labias, in Stra to the Pisanis. In Milan he decorated the palaces of the Clerici and the Archinti families with frescoes. But his two greatest creations are in Würzburg and in Madrid.

In Würzburg it was for the Greifenklau family that he decorated the Cyclopean ceiling of the main staircase with pictures of the four continents and the walls of the state room with events from Barbarossa's life. In the royal palace of Madrid the frescoes, painted between 1762 and 1774, cover a surface of several thousand square metres; here the artist, a supreme sovereign and master of space, created, with his Herculean efforts, a veritable masterpiece (Plate 38).

In his famous frescoes the flourish of trumpets and horns mingles with the sound of the organ and the sublime chorus of human voices. We can see parts of the world: golden Asia, bronze-coloured America, ivory and ebony-hued Africa; inhabitants of the animal and vegetable kingdoms face us alongside heraldic beasts: elephants and lions; Pegasus and Bucephalus; gods and goddesses, Neptune and Amphitrite, Aeolus, Cupid, Venus, Adonis and the Sun, all answering the artist's call. But side by side with them appear legionaries, knights, gladiators struggling with wild beasts, merchants, princes, mercenary chieftains, ambassadors, sailors, heroes, musicians and saints, all dressed in rich apparel, in armour and bearing weapons; they move as if they were the warriors of the greatest strategist of painting. Perspective, light and colours swirl in superlative magnificence (Plate 39).

Later all this was criticised as "festal rhetoric" or the apologetics of a flattering courtier. Tiepolo lived to experience the decline of his golden age and although he was aware of his own worth, he noted mournfully the decrease of his prestige. He had been invited to Spain and accepted the invitation, to be received and honoured in princely fashion; but towards the end of his life he had to beg for commissions. The changes in the person and favours of the king, the intrigues of the count's father-confessor, the polemics of icy Neo-Classicism—all these contributed to Tiepolo's being pushed into the background. He died in Madrid in 1770.

It is, however, an intricate matter to pursue the spread of Tiepolo's art and to follow up the traces he left behind him. Most of his disciples have sunk into oblivion and only his son Gian Domenico escaped this fate, and then only by freeing himself from his father's influence.

Gian Battista Tiepolo had many followers in Bressanone, in Bolzano and in the Tyrol; in the whole of Austria and Vienna, in Germany (in Franconia and Bavaria), as well as in Prague and the whole of Bohemia. They continued his work up to the end and, anachronistically, they did not die out until quite late in the nineteenth century. Tiepolo's only genuine heir was his son Gian Domenico (1727–1804). By heir we mean that he was the only artist who, while adopting his stupendous spiritual and formal inheritance, was able, even thirty years after his father's death, to render his style modern and topical, to bring to it a new approach and, with wise moderation, to guide it into new directions. All this freed Gian Domenico's personality from the "happy servitude", to which he seemed to owe everything. He was able to survive this servitude and even to overcome it.

Gian Domenico died on the 3rd March 1804, at the age of 77; this was 34 years after his father's death, when the son was 43 years old. He did not feel the tremendous changes taking place in the world—such as the French Revolution, Napoleon's lightning rise to fame, or the tragic end of the Serenissima. He devoted himself to depicting, in ironic vein, the customs and morals of earlier times, such as, for instance, a walk taken by the "trio" of husband, wife and lover (Plate 40); this same approach is characteristic of his works *Crier*, *Masked Minuet*, *Singer* (Kansas City), *Gondola* (Madrid, private collection), and *Barge with Oars* (Vienna). He painted scenes and episodes of rural life in a naturalistic style and abandoned the course of Venetian painting to which his father had directed him. Although he fully preserved the pictorial traditions of Venice, he neither sang the praises of saints, nor glorified families and dynasties. Gian Domenico was an innovator, who represented village life satirically and humorously. But a deep gloom filled him when he decorated for himself the rooms of the Zianigo villa which his father had longed for; here he did not heed political tempests and, although he clearly felt the approaching disintegration (1791–

1793), he nonetheless painted the *Hut of the Clowns*, and the *Coach of the Buffoons*, the *Walk* (or the *ménage à trois*), as well as the wax-works, where people queue to see the "miracles" (always the same) of the New World. Clever dogs and clowns, acrobats and monsters, the strong and the weak alike are lined up here; but they are all *clowns*, offspring of the same family. It is their fate to be the laughing-stock of themselves and of others: it is a carnival of the world, a grotesque picture gallery of life.

Rosalba Carriera (1675–1757) restricted her activity to portraiture and to her peerless technique in pastels. She was a personality who broke away from Tiepolo's trend and lived in the light that shone on her from the courts and aristocracy of half Europe.

Rosalba was born to be a daughter of art; she was influenced on the one hand by her father, a Friulian seafaring man from Chioggia, a self-taught dilettante who painted his conceptions with naive simplicity; on the other hand, by her mother, Alba di Angelo Foresti, who made Burano lace with exquisite taste.

In addition to the atmosphere of the parental home, she was helped in miniature painting by Jean Steve, a Frenchman who lived in Venice, and in the technique of pastels by the Englishman Christian Cole.

She had an emotional longing—inherited from her father—for Chioggia. This longing made her settle there, opposite the house from which the lawyer's apprentice Goldoni—who in 1728–29 was an assistant of the head of the criminal police—watched local goings-on and wrote down the gossips he heard.

Gracefulness is the most conspicuous quality of Rosalba Carriera's works. Her airy and sometimes affected forms are caressingly soft, her colours are delicate, and therefore she was sometimes considered dull and monotonous. Nor did the experts try to find out how this apparent gracefulness and frivolity was able to elicit universal approval.

But it should be remembered that as strong a fantasy and as great a moral force are needed for expressing gracefulness as are needed for conveying energy and, accordingly, one can assert that this Venetian painter filled the impalpable subtlety of her pastels, their weird fragility— 42 their very substance—with strength, and that she contributed an abiding firmness and solidity to ephemeral materials. She endowed pastels with a triumph that had never before been thought possible, she identified them with her own art, and she succeeded in creating chapters in portraiture in which emotions, thoughts and characters can be read (Plate 41). Her brushwork made her pictures graceful, although she covered everything with wax, powder and cosmetics. Her friend A.M. Zanetti pointed out that even in that frivolous century Rosalba represented herself with a laurel wreath on her head, not so much out of vanity but rather to make it clear that "...this is tragedy..." as if she were prophesying how she would end her life.

Her splendid career, full of success, adulation and honours in Paris, Dresden, Vienna, Este and Rome, came to a miserable end. Titian acquired his fame as an epic and monumental portrait painter; his art suited the world and dramas of Charles V and Pope Paul III. The personages who asked Rosalba to create intimate and delicate likenesses were no less notable in their origin and important in their destinies. They, too, were characters in tragic historical periods in three wars of succession—the Spanish, the Polish and the Austrian.

Even in her art Venice's mission lived on. Rosalba served this mission faithfully, until blindness and insanity struck the brush from her hand; she lived on as a living shadow for ten years, until the 15th April 1757.

The life of Pietro Falca, known by the name of Longhi (1702–1785), would not have surpassed mediocrity if some secret vocation had not turned his attention towards the narrative, towards intimate scenes, the "genre" which, thanks to his work, rid itself of the bad name which it had borne for several centuries. Indeed, this genre, which tended to depict trivial themes, reached the heights of pure painting. Pietro Falca did not possess the abilities to achieve this, but Pietro Longhi did. As a self-taught man he discovered in his aesthetical consciousness the possibilities which the medium offered and he then adopted the name of Longhi (Plate 42).

43 The phenomena of everyday Venice underwent a change in Longhi's

eyes; they became poetry and the essence of painting, which formed in him their Anacreon. Longhi's example is the best proof that so-called genre-painting is not *minor* painting with a limited inspiration; it is not an inferior handmaid of *major* painting, but a melody in a minor key—as in music there are two tonalities, minor and major. All this does not affect the height of inspiration and the strength of lyricism; it affects neither the poetic qualities nor their quantities. Longhi conquered the dual world of both Venice and of painting. Cultured and elegant society appreciated his seemingly idiomatic, vernacular way of expression, which struck a sophisticated note; painters and artists, on the other hand, esteemed the novelty and unusualness amidst the resounding trumpet sound and pomp which were characteristic of the century. In the issue of the 13th August, 1760 of the *Gazzetta Veneta* Gaspare Gozzi wrote: "Let us look how great is the difference between Signor Tiepoletto and Signor Longhi... The former presents some feat of arms, the meeting together in the landing of great personages; the latter a dance, an amorous adventure, or a young girl taking music lessons, and he does not represent his themes any less faithfully than does the former..." And here an inevitable comparison with Goldoni arises. The affinity between the two men, which was later widely acclaimed as a new discovery, was felt by Goldoni himself, who praised it in his famous sonnet as a genuine *Wahlverwandtschaft*:

> *Longhi, thou who summons my sister-muse*
> *with thy brush seeking the truth.*

Indeed Goldoni, from depicting mummers and their like, rose to a level where he created and explored man the individual, the personality. Thus he progressed from the *commedia dell'arte* to comedy representing morals, manners and characters. Longhi had set out from the Olympus of Neo-Classicists but included in his works the observations of his time. He showed how patricians, peasants and charlatans lived and, taking a bold step forwards, he broke with traditions and rejected the taste of his own period. He made perplexing statements about the trend of Realism, 44 which were not only the premises of ideas of contemporary and of later critics and even of literary wits from Goldoni to Gozzi, but confronted the Neo-Classic argument with a new attitude. Canova too got involved in the argument, but, most laudably, Gian Domenico Tiepolo and young Longhi joined sides. Discerning writers and critics of the age recognized Longhi at once. Alessandro Longhi stated: "My father painted small pictures of bourgeois pastimes; he took his themes from reality and this was how he achieved his effect." According to G.A. Moschini: "He changed his style when he began to paint small figures in a manner then new and since then unknown..."

The fact that the critics of those times so greatly emphasized the smallness of the figures may have caused a misunderstanding with regard to the narrowing-down of the poetic-pictorial world. We may call this world a microcosm, but the infinite variety of the ways of life represented nevertheless made it a reflection of new social reality. With uncanny exactitude the art of portraiture appears in these representations. True, the pictures are small, but they are not miniatures and they interpret characters with amazing faithfulness. This can be seen in the observations of the human face both in group portraits and in drawing-room likenesses; the Sagredo family or family concerts offer good examples of these qualities.

There is a well-known saying: if somebody wants to know what a Venetian lady is doing in any hour of the day, he should ask Longhi and he will receive an answer. The depicting of the everyday life of society is more intimate and homely than that of contemporary French artists, such as Lancret and Chardin; it is freer and more animated than that of Flemish or Dutch artists, because in Longhi's series about peasant life people never appear in such disorder and confusion as they do in paintings representing *kermesses*. The gentle or repressed smile is sometimes ironical, sometimes malicious, but it is never hypocritical.

As far as the naturalness of the scenes is concerned, some scholars have pointed to signs that linked Pietro Longhi in his early years with Crespi and Piazzetta. Such are, for example, *The Flea-Hunting Girl* or *After the Bath*.

Pietro's son, Alessandro Longhi (1733–1813), was also a significant painter. Naturalness and an interest in the life of ordinary people are basic features of his art. He soon freed himself from his father's influence, although in some portraits the touch of Pietro's hand and that of his son's are easily confused. After some hesitating beginnings Alessandro devoted his whole work to portraiture. His art is of historic importance; on the one hand because of the artistic value of the pictures and, on the other, because there were outstanding personalities among his sitters, or among those who visited the studio of the master who at no time left his own country.

He painted the likeness of Carlo Goldoni, of Cimarosa, during the short and sad period of his exile in Venice, before he died in his house in Campo Sant'Angelo in 1813. He painted the Pisanis, the chief judges, the highest officials, the Contarinis, Da Mula and Father Lodoli, architect and theoretician. Among these works the most notable is the portrait of Jacopo Gradenigo, head of the Admiralty (Padua, Museum; Plate 43).

His work is mentioned as that of an "innovator", because, before Goya, "he invented green, red and blue portraits, and did not even scruple to include in them his father's artful embarrassment... even in life-size portraits; he painted them without bothering about outlines" (Roberto Longhi).

Like his father and like Gian Domenico Tiepolo, he was also a Venetian painter in his brushwork. Although he was a contemporary and compatriot of Canova's, to the very end he quietly but unflinchingly resisted Classicism which, because of Canova's work, reached its zenith at that time.

Another trend of taste, the *veduta*, an exceedingly important genre of Settecento painting in the Veneto, has a quite different historical and aesthetical significance. It has to be sharply demarcated from earlier and from contemporary landscape painting. To make the distinction clearer and more comprehensible we are going to call this latter "terrestrial" landscape painting. This trend drew on Claude Lorrain's example.

Up to Pannini there had always been some convention, the observance of some rule in *vedutismo* with landscapes or ruins.

46

But the Venetian master sings, in terms of his own pictorial idiom, the praises of what he has seen—from this is derived the name of the genre, *veduta*, that is to say, the thing seen—always some part of his beloved Venice.

The Venetian painter of *vedute* never "took photographs", he was a poet, the poet of a reality that no one was ever able to understand, to approach and to represent as he was. And yet, what a host of artists—from Turner to Segantini—came to Venice on a pictorial pilgrimage from all parts of the world.

The two notions: *veduta* and Venice coincide in one name: Canaletto, both the first and the second of this name.

Gentile Bellini's and Carpaccio's painting had already forecast the possibilities of the *veduta*. Venetian landscape painting started with Marco Ricci and went on to Zuccarelli and Zais. The *veduta*, on the other hand, reached perfection in the works of the two Canalettos and to some extent in those of Francesco Guardi.

In creating *vedute* new aesthetic points asserted themselves. Geometrical perspective was abandoned and nature was rediscovered; live and noble colours again glittered crystal-clear; but gold-leaf or optical tricks and technical and geometrical calculations and measurements were missing. Poetic magic made what was exact uncertain, it made outlines and architectural forms vibrate by identifying them with atmosphere, with luminous mists and with translucent air and—a miracle had been performed.

Baroque rhetoric, in a stupendous *fortissimo*, had extolled the superficial values of perspective and had resorted to extremes; it aimed at inferior stage effects; it dazzled the spectator with halves, apotheoses, the vaults of heaven and swirling bodies. It was not due to chance that Antonio Canal had started as a stage-designer, but then turned his back upon this work and fixed his eyes upon the *Urbs picta*. It was there that he received guidance and inspiration, discovering a new dimension of distance, and a new way of seeing things in perspective.

The first masters working in the magic circle of the lagoons audaciously complemented nature with art. Giovanni Antonio Canal (1697–1768) had made this vision his own to such an extent that when he emigrated to London he painted northern landscapes too as if they had been Venetian; the second Canaletto, Bernardo Bellotto, reacted in the same way in old Vienna, in Dresden and on the banks of the Vistula.

But it was not only the youthful experiences of Giovanni Antonio Canaletto that were enriched first in Rome and then in London. From the Eternal City—where he worked particularly industriously—he brought with him the memory of the "painters of ruins" and of the works of art of ancient Rome.

Canaletto's œuvre was widespread and the limits of this summary are very restricted, thus we cannot mention his paintings by their titles. However, in order to bring the reader nearer to his art we must also point to his extraordinarily interesting drawings and engravings. The importance of drawings is not only the fact that they "prepare" the painting, but also that they approach reality and they are acceptable representations. These drawings are complete; they are mostly pen-drawings and are thus indelible and irrevocable. They soar freely, buoyantly, their tones are accurate, and their lights and shades achieve the effects of a painting. They are as vigorous and solid as the engravings; indeed, they can even be taken for the first prints of an engraving. They are as constructive and strong as Piranesi's most eminent creations, but they are, at the same time, as much the work of a painter as are Guardi's best works.

Bernardo Bellotto (1720–1780) was the nephew of Antonio Canal, the son of one of his sisters; he assumed the name of his uncle Canaletto. In the whole history of Italian painting there was never an identity of names more justified, natural and acceptable than in his case. Bellotto set out together with his uncle on a career of *veduta* painting; in the course of his years of study he went forward with his master, to such an extent that sometimes we are not sure to whom to attribute a youthful work. But Bellotto was never a blind imitator.

His sense of space is essentially different from his uncle's. Examined from the point of view of pure painting the new features, which appear in his landscapes of Lombardy, increasingly gain ground; the light is stronger than Canal's mother-of-pearl subtle lambency; definite light is sometimes characterized by a stronger colouring of deeper shadows, because he used *terra di Siena* and various brown pigments. Canal's characteristic airiness grew heavy; on the other hand Bellotto's perspective and pictorial construction was filled with vigour. It was this trait which forecast the period of his activity, soon to begin, which is called his Saxon-Viennese period: from 1747 onwards he began painting the *vedute* of Dresden in the court of Frederick Augustus. Then he went to Vienna (1759–1760) to work for Maria Theresa, Chancellor Kaunitz (Plate 45) and Count Harrach, and to record *vedute* of Mozart's and Haydn's age, of Beethoven's and Schubert's Romantic times.

At that time the Seven Years' War was raging. In 1760 Prussian cannon fire destroyed Bellotto's house and studio in Dresden, as well as his works. Embittered by setbacks, he moved to Munich in 1761 and then started out for St. Petersburg. On the way he stopped in Warsaw and there he remained. It was in that city that he made his final home.

Just after settling down there he began painting his Warsaw *vedute* in 1767 and he continued working on them up to his death in 1780. That is why he is known as the painter of Warsaw. In these pictures the soul of the Venetian *vedutist* came to be filled with new passions—as if he had had a foreboding of the future. Together with his uncle he was "the painter of Venice", but he found a second home in Warsaw. This he faithfully depicted and he could not foresee what shining fame his life, so full of vicissitudes, was to gain from this new citizenship.

Anyone who saw the ruins of this heroic city after the Second World War, who has seen it rebuilt and who has admired the devotion with which first the former historical centre was restored and only then were the residential parts of the town rebuilt, will understand the role cast by destiny for the Venetian painter. It is said that if Venice disappeared her entire life could be seen in the paintings of Canaletto (and of Guardi). Warsaw was in very fact destroyed and for long lived on only in the image left by Bellotto.

49 His uncle found numerous pupils and followers in London, Bellotto in

Warsaw. But in Italy, too, a great many artists joined the trend. Their last representative, Giovanni Migliara, died in 1837.

The other course of so-called real landscape painting started with Marco Ricci, who is considered the paragon of the style. But this definition cannot exclude all that the great artists said and painted from their observation of nature at the end of the Quattrocento and the beginning of the Cinquecento. Cima da Conegliano, Giambellino, Giorgione and Titian played an important part in the Venetian interpretation of scenery and the beauties of nature.

Two names stand out among the many landscape painters: those of Zuccarelli and Zais. Francesco Zuccarelli (1702–1778) was a Tuscan by birth. French *galanterie* influenced his art. Giuseppe Zais (1709–1784) was a native of the Belluno region. But both of them were brought up on the painting of the Veneto and on Ricci's art. Their approach is similar; they were both fond of decorative, pastoral landscapes and they both placed the same figures in the same landscape: rustics, shepherds and shepherdesses, women washing their laundry in brooks, fishermen, hunters and horsemen (Plate 46). They painted bridges and little waterfalls, ramparts and pebbled riverbeds, banks and clearings enlivened by dances and games, as well as pastures, mills and huts. Originally Zais was the harder and more tempestuous character, but sometimes he approached the way in which Zuccarelli, with his urbaner and softer manner, represented a more sophisticated society and even tolerated mythological themes *(The Rape of Europa)*. Zais was nearer to the peasantry and drew his inspiration from a simpler, more bucolic life. We may also say that Zais created eclogues and Zuccarelli madrigals. Thus, in spite of their similarities, their styles assist us in distinguishing between them. Zais's brushwork was freer, his features were broader, more impetuous and better suited to expressing the essential.

We have reached the epilogue of the thousand years' history of the Serenissima. Everything that centuries of heroic struggle and tenacity had brought to full flower collapsed in ruins.

Celebrations and festivities followed one after another, but the majestic scene of the Republic's pomp was now nothing but the background to its last carnival. The period ended in moral decay. The most characteristic figure of this disintegrating society was Giacomo Casanova, the spy.

Honest Goldoni, the portrayer of morals, seems to have been unwilling to watch this sad twilight, this humiliating catastrophe. He therefore moved to Paris, where he died in the most passionate and most terrible days of the Revolution. There he thought back to Venice, where children were attacking their parents and were destroying the heraldic lions of St. Mark.

Venetian painting watched the state's dying agony as if from outside; it came to an end with a *finale* of lyrical beauty. This paradoxical phenomenon can be summarized in one name, that of Francesco Guardi (1712–1793). His painting and all that he created in his workshop together with his brother Gianantonio (1699–1760) was important even from a historical point of view.

And yet their critical rehabilitation is due to our own age. In 1913 Gino Fogolari uncovered from the archives of the Accademia of Venice the name of Gianantonio Guardi, Francesco's brother. The name was brought to light after over a century's oblivion. Previously the two masters had been criticized sternly, pompously or non-committally; because of the unfortunate heritage of Neo-Classicism, they had even been despised. Today the two names and the two œuvres shine in a new light, and we simply cannot understand this lack of appreciation, this injustice.

I shall spare the reader the complicated problems of the authorship of different pictures among the numerous masters belonging to the Guardi family, and the arguments about which of the two greatest artists had painted certain works, for this is outside the framework of our survey. I will restrict myself to giving an outline of Gianantonio and Francesco Guardi's œuvre.

It is debatable what the role of the two brothers in the family rivalry—essentially reduced to these two names—was; the statement that one of them was a figure painter and the other a *vedutist* is also rather arbitrary. It must be enough to remember that it is certain that Francesco painted pictures with figures, altar-pieces; this is made clear by all those works he produced after Gianantonio's death.

The discovery of the artistic values of the Guardis gave rise to the view that their art was "revolutionary"; family talent had, however, been deeply rooted in Venetian traditions.

On the basis of the few works that can unhesitatingly be attributed to Gianantonio, he seems to have been more faithful to tradition than Francesco and not so "elevated". Nevertheless, in my opinion, Gianantonio can be regarded as the first teacher of his brother, who was 13 years his junior. It was he who launched his younger brother on the course of painting, he who ran the business side of the workshop. This workshop operated virtually like a family co-operative, and Niccolò may have worked closely with it; Giacomo, too, Francesco's son, the last craftsman of the family, cannot have been without contact with it.

The collaboration began about 1730, or in the decade following, when the parish church of Vigo d'Anaunia was being restored. The fruit of the joint work of the Guardi brothers is the famous altar-piece of the Belvedere of Grado (Aquileia), after 1746 (Plate 47); the large rose-windows of Vigo d'Anaunia. The altar-piece of Roncegno (Trento) was completed after Gianantonio's death. No one doubts that they are joint creations, although there are contradictory views about the degree to which each contributed.

Two important panel paintings deserve special mention, not only on account of their artistic value but also because they give a faithful picture of the morals of the period. They are the *Nuns' Living-Room* and the *Ridotto* (Gambling Club) in the Palazzo Rezzonico in Venice. I for one would support Gianantonio's authorship of these easel paintings, whereas in the series representing the story of young Tobias and the Archangel Raphael in the Church of San Raffaele Arcangelo I would suppose a collaboration. The spectator is almost dazzled by the brilliant handling, by the gracefully fluid strokes of the brush and by the diamond-like glitter of colours. It was this collaboration that gave birth to the style whose most significan representative Francesco Guardi was. Indeed, he was able to present in a miraculous synthesis the art of Veronese and Tintoretto, of Fetti and Solimena, of Ricci and Piazzetta and of his contemporary Longhi—but in the course of his amazing development he was subject to closer impacts, too: those of Marco Ricci and of the diabolical Genoese Magnasco. Nowadays the Guardi brothers, and Francesco in particular, have been granted the rank due to them; modern criticism appreciates their true worth. But we must warn the reader against wrongly identifying this art with Rococo *galanterie*, with salon literature and with frivolousness and extravagance. Francesco Guardi's painting is in no way superficial or routine. His seeming airiness is like the strength of Mozart, which permeates the torture of creation and raises even the most threadbare and fraudulent craftsmanship to the height of elevated lyrical expression.

It is due to this strength that the pictorial material becomes transubstantiated and ethereally weightless, soaring in the blazing fire of colours and light. Light shot through with sparkling and tempestuous flames, expresses this strength. The painting is extraordinarily airy and in it the brush strokes the canvas and leaves behind spots of colour. Passion is ablaze everywhere, the pure lyrical passion of colour, a passion that seizes the painter, the timid and isolated man who refuses invitations and never leaves Venice, who endures unpopularity at the same Accademia which honoured Angelica Kauffmann.

Guardi represented the end of Venetian painting in the double circle of light formed by light itself and by the spots of colour made by the brush. In this strong and delicate, highly sensitive and impalpable element the sense of weight disappears.

From the political events of battle-scenes to be seen in the Doges' Palace, from the reality of court and state portraits we pass on to the nameless unposed masses which crowd the Piazza and Piazzetta, which had become choreographic stages. For Guardi, sea captains had vanished before Campoformio, and so had individualities. They do not appear even on the minute scale to which they had been reduced by Pietro Longhi. The community, the masses, represented only by some summary, quick strokes of the brush, had ousted haughty personages from these stages.

Guardi resplendently depicts the rush towards disaster. But if we look at his works more closely, we shall see that they radiate a foreboding sorrow

53

—almost a last farewell (Plate 48). The painter takes leave of happiness. How right Lionello Venturi is: "Guardi's art is often imbued with sadness, with some sweet sorrow, by which he seems to predict the end of the world."

Pietro Longhi represented the everyday life of patricians, of the bourgeoisie and of the peasantry, and the grey monotony of their uneventful lives, with superb pictorial taste and with subtle irony. Domenico Tiepolo showed us satires of people, of hunchbacks and clowns, with gentle and resigned bitterness. But Francesco Guardi was a keener observer than his two contemporaries; he sensed that the marvellous history, whose last chronicler and heir was he himself—a fact he was well aware of—had come to an end. He died on the 1st of January, 1793. A month later, on the 6th February, Carlo Goldoni also died in Paris.

Francesco Guardi ended his life in misery. He died at Campo della Madonnetta in San Canciano, in the small home where he had modestly lived and worked. With his death the golden age of Venetian painting came to an end.

BIBLIOGRAPHY

C. RIDOLFI: *Le Maraviglie dell' Arte-ovvero degli Illustri pittori veneziani dello Stato.* Venice, 1648

M. BOSCHINI: *La Carta del Navegar pittoresco.* Venice, 1660

M. BOSCHINI: *Le Ricche Miniere della Pittura Veneziana.* Venice, 1674

A. M. ZANETTI: *Della pittura veneziana e delle opere pubbliche dei veneziani Maestri.* Libri 5. Venice, 1771

E. ZINEMAN: *Die Landschaft in der venezianischen Malerei.* Leipzig, 1893

B. BERENSON: *Venetian Painters of the Renaissance.* New York, 1894

L. VENTURI: *Le origini della pittura veneziana.* Venice, 1907

L. TESTI: *La storia della pittura veneziana.* Bergamo, 1909

G. B. SACK: *Giambattista und Giandomenico Tiepolo.* Hamburg, 1910

L. CROWE – G.B. CAVALCASELLE: *A History of Painting in North Italy.* London, 1912

L. PLANISCIG: *Venezianische Bildhauer der Renaissance.* Vienna, 1921

H. WOSS: "Studien zur venezianischen Vedutenmalerei des XVIII. Jahrhunderts". *Repertorium für Kunstwissenschaft,* 1926

D. VON HALDEN: *Handzeichnungen von G.B. Tiepolo.* Munich, 1927

G. FIOCCO: *La pittura veneziana del seicento e settecento.* Verona–Florence, 1929

G. DE LOGU: *Pittori veneti minori del settecento.* Venice, 1930

D. VON HALDEN: *Die Zeichnungen von A. Canal.* Vienna, 1930

G. GRONAU: *Tizian.* Stuttgart, 1930

V. MOSCHINI: *La pittura italiana del '700.* Florence, 1931

A. SPANN: *Palma il Vecchio.* Leipzig, 1932

G.M. RICHTER: *Giorgio da Castelfranco.* Chicago, 1937

A.E. BRINCKMANN: *Die Kunst der Rokoko.* Berlin, 1940

L. DUSSLER: *Sebastiano del Piombo.* Basle, 1942

E. VAN DER BERKEN: *Tintoretto.* Munich, 1942

R. PALLUCCHINI: *La pittura veneziana del '500.* Novara, 1944

R. PALLUCCHINI: *Cinque secoli di pittura veneziana.* Venice, 1945

55

R. LONGHI: *Viatico per cinque secoli di pittura veneziana.* Florence, 1946

E. ARSLAN: *Il concetto di "luminismo" e la pittura veneta barocca.* Milan, 1946

H. TIETZE: *Tintoretto.* London, 1948

K.T. PARKER: *The Drawings of Antonio Canaletto at Windsor Castle.* London, 1948

F.B. WATSON: *Canaletto.* London, 1949

K. SCHEFFLER: *Venezianische Malerei.* Berlin, 1949

W.C. CONSTABLE: *Venetian Paintings.* London, 1949

H. TIETZE: *Titian, the Paintings and Drawings.* London, 1950

J. DUPONT–F. MATHEY: *Le Dix-septième siècle.* Geneva, 1951

L. COLETTI: *Pittura veneta del '400.* Novara, 1953

M. VALSECCHI: *La pittura veneziana.* Milan, 1954

B. BERENSON: *Lorenzo Lotto.* Milan, 1955

T. PIGNATTI: *Pittura veneziana del '500.* Bergamo, 1957

G. DE LOGU: *Pittura veneziana dal XIV al XVII secolo.* Bergamo, 1958

T. PIGNATTI: *Pittura veneziana del '400.* Bergamo, 1959

MOJZER, M.: *Az északolasz cinquecento* [The North-Italian Cinquecento]. Budapest, 1960

CZOBOR, Á.: *Barokk művészet Itáliában* [Baroque Art in Italy]. Budapest, 1961

M. BONICATTI: *Aspetti dell'umanesimo nella pittura veneta dal 1455 al 1515.* Rome, 1964

C. DONZELLI–G.M. PILO: *I pittori del '600 veneto.* Florence, 1967

C. DONZELLI: *I pittori veneti del '700.* Florence, 1967

GARAS, K.: *A velencei settecento festészete* [Eighteenth Century Venetian Paintings]. Budapest, 1968

A. BLUNT: *Artistic Theory in Italy 1450–1600.* Oxford, 1973

E. WIND: *Giorgione's Tempesta.* Oxford, 1973

G. ROBERTSON: *Giovanni Bellini.* Oxford, 1973

E. PANOFSKY: *Problems in Titian. Mostly Iconographic.* Princeton, 1973

H.E. WETHEY: *The Paintings of Titian.* London, 1973

GARAS, K.: *Olasz reneszánsz portrék* [Italian Renaissance Portraits]. Budapest, 1973

LIST OF PLATES

PLATES

GENTILE BELLINI
1429–1507

I

CATERINA CORNARO, QUEEN OF CYPRUS

About 1500. Museum of Fine Arts, Budapest
Oil on wood, 63 × 48 cm

One of the few authentic portraits of the Queen of Cyprus; there is one other in the Avogadro Collection, presented by the Queen as a wedding gift to one of her ladies-in-waiting, and a third, which is supposed to be Bellini's likeness of her in his *Miracle of the Cross*, with Caterina painted bottom left among her handmaids.

The three works have some iconographic features in common: the Queen is portrayed in all of them at a mature age, wearing the same headgear, her crowned head surmounted by a veil of flimsy fabric, which reveals a time-worn face. It takes a stretch of imagination to recognize in the old lady the celebrated Caterina Cornaro, far-famed for her beauty and intelligence, the spouse of James of Lusignan, King of Cyprus.

Gentile Bellini, Jacopo Bellini's direct heir, excelled equally in portrait-painting and in scenes of vast brushwork, evocative of the "feel" of the times and foreshadowing the spirit of that Venice of the 1500's which marked an unmistakable moment in history. His fame as a portraitist spread far and wide beyond the borders of his country, earning him a mission as official painter of the State of the Doges to paint a portrait of Mehmet II, the Conqueror.

2

ANTONELLO DA MESSINA
1430–1479

ALTAR-PIECE OF SAN CASSIANO (fragments)

1475–76. Kunsthistorisches Museum, Vienna
Oil on wood. Centre-piece (The Madonna) 115 × 65 cm; left wing (Saint Nicolas
of Bari and Magdalen) 55.9 × 35 cm; right wing (St. Ursula and Dominic) 56.8 × 35.6 cm

Little is known about the artist, except for what has been handed down by
Vasari, and later by Ridolfi. The works are attributed to Messina above all
because of the strength of the new style of painting, claimed to have been
inspired by a journey to Flanders. Still, the artist had his first grounding in the
South of Italy. It was certainly here that he brushed shoulders with the
Flemish painters and grafted onto his painting a new visual dimension, using
colours to broaden space into more airy vistas.
In 1475 he was staying in Venice and the San Cassiano altar-piece came as
a sequel to a series of works, including the Antwerp crucifixion, and a number of portraits. Designed round a novel architectonic skeleton, this canvas
came to be the inevitable model and paragon for all the prestigious painters
of the age, from Bellini, with his San Giobbe altar-piece, to Giorgione, the
painter of the Castelfranco altar, and Alvise Vivarini, whose altar-piece was
destroyed in the Kaiser Friedrich Museum at Berlin in 1945.
This particular work of Antonello's, which had so significant an influence on
his artistic career, and also on the history of subsequent Venetian painting,
disappeared from the Church of San Cassiano in the first decades of the
17th century. Ridolfi mentions it in 1648. Reduced to fragments, it reappeared
in the collection of the Archduke Leopold William in Brussels, and was
attributed to Giovanni Bellini. About this time, Teniers made copies and
engravings of them. In 1700 three or so of the large fragments found their
way to Vienna. The two side-wings remained unrecognized until 1928, when
they were put on show by Wilde. The Madonna was displayed, attributed now
to Bellini, now to Boccaccino (Wickhoff, 1893 and Berenson, 1916–17); the
latter was the first to identify in this picture the centre-piece of the San Cassiano
altar. Finally Wilde managed to trace the two lateral fragments and tried to
reconstruct the whole (1929).

GIOVANNI BELLINI
1428/30–1516

3

ALTAR-PIECE IN THE CHURCH OF SAN GIOBBE

About 1487. Gallerie dell'Accademia, Venice
Oil on wood, 471 × 258 cm. Signed: Joannes Bellinus

The painting, made for the Venetian Church of San Giobbe, decorated an altar, which followed up its painted architecture in terms of stone, and represents the Madonna with the Infant, with St. Francis, St. John the Baptist and St. Job on her left, St. Dominic, St. Sebastian and St. Louis on her right, and musicking angels below.

The design is presumably instinct with the influence of Antonello (see his San Cassiano altar-piece), who worked in Venice in 1475–76 and from whom Bellini must have learned the technique of oil-painting. Superimposed on this indisputable influence are the obvious humanistic undertones, and the heritage of Mantegna and the Tuscans (Piero della Francesca). The pyramidal composition, which is a clear-cut revolution against the former design of altar-pieces, places the Madonna in the apex of the picture. Action would thus seem to be afloat, with the minor figures motionless in an attitude of contemplation and prayer. The tranquility that inspires the figurative order of this sacred tableau expresses the loftiest sense of the genius of the age.

GIOVANNI BELLINI

4

SACRA CONVERSAZIONE (THE ALLEGORY OF SOULS IN PURGATORY)

1490–1505. Galleria degli Uffizi, Florence
Oil on wood, 73 × 119 cm

The painting was attributed to Giorgione up to 1871, when Cavalcaselle definitively showed it to be Giovanni Bellini's work, and art critics generally agreed to accept it as such. Its theme is doubtful and there have always been arguments about its authentic name.

Earlier views held that the subject-matter was drawn from "Le pélerinage de l'âme", a little poem written at the end of the 14th century by Guillaume de Deguilleville. Niccolò Rasmo disputed this claim (1946); in his opinion the representation fits into the framework of a "saintly colloquy". Later this hypothesis was refuted by Verdier (1953–1954) and Braunfels (1956), the former seeing it as an allegory of commiseration and justice, the latter as an image of Paradise.

With the neo-paganism of Venetian painting in the early part of the 16th century breaking forth in this work, there is a connection with a development in culture which is better contemplated within the hermetic world of a humanist "temple" than in an open *ambiance*, hallowed as this may be. A work of the master's maturity, it marks in him a meeting-point in time of all the currents of experience that made him what he was. He handles this fullness freely, impregnates it with a new mysticism, a consciousness in thought that by now links him to the custom born of a renewed philosophy. This is certainly the educated Venetian background from which sprang such literary masterpieces as *Hypnerotomachia Poliphili* published by Manuzio (1499) and illustrated with xylographs, which give a hint of being inspired by the master (Pignatti, 1969). The scene bursts upon the view within the perspective of the marble floor closed with a balustrade: the work consists of two parts symbolizing the dual colloquy. Three-dimensional perspective below and naturalistic landscape above, the whole is populated with mythological figures and suffused with the unreal light of a new vitalizing emotion.

GIOVANNI BELLINI

FEAST OF THE GODS

5

1514. National Gallery, Washington
Oil on canvas, 170 × 188 cm

The signed and dated work ("Joannes Bellinus Venetus MDXIV") was displayed in Alfonso d'Este's little alabaster-lined study or closet in his Ferrara castle. Originating from Bellini's mature period, it was done, in all probability, for Isabella d'Este; accordingly, he must have begun it a good deal earlier than the date it bears. Some critics assign it to 1509 (Wind, 1958 and Pallucchini, 1959). By subjecting the canvas to an X-ray examination, Walker identified three coats of paint, notably: Bellini's original, a later one in Dossi's manner, and, lastly, one by Titian. In fact Pallucchini has pointed out that "several changes in the figures can be attributed to Titian", but nonetheless Bellini's concept is clearly conveyed in the limpidly incisive character conferred by the drawing, and highlighted by the shifting colours, so much so that, as Vasari observed (1568), "there is a distinct feel of Dürer's influence." Thus "these alterations have marred none of Bellini's crystal-clear poetry, which makes the *Feast of the Gods* one of his masterpieces" (Pignatti, 1969).

The work, which old age compelled him to leave unfinished, is certainly of great importance for Bellini and for Venetian painting, with its then current tendency to forge closer links with the culture of the age.

6

GIOVANNI BELLINI

FEAST OF THE GODS (detail)

The spirit of the new times is clearly evoked in a scene animated by a mythography of personages: forest deities, centaurs and unicorns transfigure the new patrons' sophisticated modernities. At once the final apotheosis of the first Venetian Renaissance period and a gateway to the triumphant new dream of the Cinquecento, this last work of Bellini's merges Giorgione and Titian by reason of their cultural affinity.

7

VITTORE CARPACCIO
1460/65–1526

ST. AUGUSTINE IN HIS STUDY

1502. Oratorio della Scuola di San Giorgio degli Schiavoni, Venice
Oil on canvas, 141 × 210 cm

Carpaccio, who was reared on Antonello da Messina's plasticity of forms and tectonic spatial effects, by a minute and imaginative scrutiny of reality transcends Gentile Bellini's bald documentary purpose and turns an adept hand to translating any experience and vision into pictorial terms on his canvas. Even in the St. Ursula Histories he made his imagery plausible by accurately depicting every scene in which the fantasy-ridden and the tangible fuse in a fabled submarine world. The same can be said of his cycle in San Giorgo degli Schiavoni, which is the summit of full maturity. His *St. Augustine in His Study* testifies to a lynx-eyed perception of every tiny detail: everything is minutely defined with a sort of Flemish thoroughness, and placed in a context that conveys a feel of the entire Italian perspective vision, "providing the stylistic groundwork of the painting" (Pignatti, 1966). Carpaccio limns the ideal interior of a humanist saint's study, where a pervasive mood of calm and serenity informs every object, punctuated with realistic detail "to set off a character at once saintly and secular in a harmonious cadence" (Perocco, 1961), with only the stark light falling in from the window disrupting the sequence, and freezing the saint's gesture, to confer a sense of waiting on the entire scene.

GIORGIONE (GIORGIO DA CASTELFRANCO)
c. 1477–1510

8

MADONNA AND CHILD ENTHRONED BETWEEN ST. FRANCIS AND ST. LIBERALIS

About 1505. Castelfranco Veneto, Cathedral
Oil on wood, 200 × 152 cm

The altar-piece was, in all probability, commissioned by the Condottiere Tuzio Costanzo in memory of his son Matteo, who died in 1504: the Costanzo coat-of-arms can be seen on the base of the Virgin's throne. It can almost certainly be dated to 1505 (Ridolfi, 1648): although it is not signed, the authorship is made indisputable by Giorgione's individual technique in laying on delicately shaded coats of paint without any underlying scaffolding from a drawing. The traditional scheme of composition is lightened by the novel use of such elements as the throne and the landscape, which takes up a good portion of the background.

9

GIORGIONE

MADONNA AND CHILD ENTHRONED BETWEEN ST. FRANCIS AND ST. LIBERALIS (detail)

This is at once a lay and a religious scene and its structure is related to Antonello's altar-piece painted in San Cassiano. Already the pictorial signs appear of a composition that breaks freely into the open air, and turns the spectator's attention not so much to the sacred scene of the altar or the centrally-placed Madonna, but rather outwards, in that striving after light and nature which will be the dominant characteristic of the forthcoming Venetian mode of painting.

THE TEMPEST

Gallerie dell'Accademia, Venice
Oil on canvas, 82×73 cm

This is one of the few works which is held by the connoisseurs to be incontest-ably Giorgione's handiwork. But they disagree about its origin and theme. In the Vendramin collection (1569) it appears as *Mercury and Isis*. Michiel, who saw the painting at the Vendramins' home in 1530, records it, giving this brief description: "The landscape on the canvas, with the tempest, the gipsy woman and the soldier, is the work of Zorzi of Castelfranco." Some date it even earlier than 1500, others feel it ought to be put later. On the theme, one of the most likely and sensible interpretations comes from Battisti (Emporium, 1957), who discovers the myth of Io in the scene: the nymph, under the protection of Mercury (the soldier) suckles her son Epaphus, fathered by Jupiter, the lightning flashing across the sky. Battisti says: "In the Venetian milieu of the first Cinquecento period there is a tendency to depict mythological scenes without any archaeological frame of reference... in this context, the pagan myths assume, as it were, the stamp of perpetual recur-rences." Yet nature is invariably the protagonist of the picture, blending figures and scenery in a Pan-pervaded atmosphere, turning both into primor-dial emblems. An X-ray examination discovered a nude figure of a woman immersed in the river; in the first sketch it appeared in the place of the young man on the left. This would seem to suggest that the subject-matter was not "inevitable", but rather that Giorgione was in quest of some ideal aesthetic formulation.

GIORGIONE

PORTRAIT OF ANTONIO BROCCARDO (?)

Museum of Fine Arts, Budapest
Oil on canvas, 72.5 × 54 cm

The authorship of this work of Giorgione's is very much disputed; recently some critics (Coletti, Fiocco) have attributed it to Pordenone, relying upon the analogy with the Onigo portrait (Richmond, Cook Collection). Accordingly, the person represented would not be "Antonius Broccardus Marri Filius", as the legend on the border (undoubtedly a later addition) would have it, nor, as claimed by others, Vittore Cappello, who died in 1466. Iconography apart, this painting is one of the wittiest portraits of Venetian art, although the colour and form are not generally considered worthy of Giorgione. According to A. Venturi, of all the works executed in Giorgione's manner, this one is most closely akin to the Castelfranco master. Later Berenson placed it firmly and definitively amongst the master's works. This portrait has always attracted the interest of the foremost critics; their views are summarized by Longhi and Garas (1961) who, rejecting any other hypothesis, definitely assign it to Giorgione; they take their stand on the latest X-ray examination, which corrects the angle of the eye and modifies some of the facial lineaments, as the superimposed layers and retouchings might have tampered with the proper reading of the artistic intent.

TITIAN (TIZIANO VECELLIO)
1488/90–1576

BACCHANALIA OR THE ANDRIANS

About 1518. Museo del Prado, Madrid
Oil on canvas, 175 × 193 cm

This work, like the *Feast of Venus*, also in the Prado, and *Bacchus and Ariadne*, National Gallery, London, was part of the pictorial décor in Alfonso d'Este's cabinet in the Castle of Ferrara.

Tradition has it that this painting, together with the *Feast of Venus*, was presented to Philip IV by the Roman Niccolò Ludovisi; later, at the end of his tenure as a Roman viceroy, the Count of Monterey took it to Spain. The portrayal was, in all probability, commissioned at the instance of Tommaso Mosti, a Ferrara man of letters and Duke Alfonso's confidant.

The scene unfolds amidst the usual imagery of Bacchus' orgiastic and frenzied drunkenness, yet with an undercurrent of the lyrical chords of humanist poetry inspired by Philostratos and Catullus, an influence of the classics produced in Venice at Aldo Manuzio's printing workshop.

The flow and movement of the composition are conjured up by the alternation of song and libation. The interposed human shapes, moving centrifugally, are the focal-point of the entertainment, at once the epitome and the theme of the work. The trees against the background of a white sky create a sort of backdrop of spontaneous and primal beauty. In the opposite corner, as in Bellini's *Feast of the Gods*, "a limply recumbent Bacchante's sensual nude body seems to herald the Pardo Venus" (cf. De Logu: *Titian*, 1950). This is the period of the highly adept artist, in which the glorification of ancient myths revive in a renewed classicism, which bears the mark of a naturalism of ideal serenity.

TITIAN

VENUS OF URBINO

1538. Galleria degli Uffizi, Florence
Oil on canvas, 165 × 119 cm

Vasari claims to have seen the painting in the family clothing chamber of the Dukes of Urbino. Later, in 1631, the Della Rovere family inherited it. Titian worked at this painting early in 1538 on behalf of Guidobaldo Della Rovere, Duke of Camerino, and future successor to the Urbino Dukedom.
In 1963, Reff devoted a lengthy iconological treatise to this work and came to the conclusion that the lady portrayed was Eleonora Gonzaga, wife of Francesco Della Rovere, Duke of Urbino. (The Duke died in the same year, 1538.)
The question of identity apart, there is a clear reference intended by Titian to Giorgione's *Sleeping Venus*, and so to the literary and artistic notions that influenced his predecessor. It shows him as an adherent of Bembo, the humanistic hints to be found in Poliphilos, Ficino's intellectual world and Almorò Barbaro's neo-Aristotelianism.
A masterpiece from Titian's mature period, it shows the seeds from which Venetian painting was later to blossom out. There is, for instance, the superb balance of light and colour achieved here by shades of red diagonally spreading across the canvas. The light seems set into an unreal immobility caused by the perspective and the lines on the floor lead out of the window into the evening air of an endless horizon. The balance of the colouristic relationship between outside and interior is plainly separated by a subdued green, giving the scene a vertical background and embracing the nude Venus, whose voluptuously shining body sinks into quiescence.

VENUS OF URBINO (detail)

In the corner of the room two servant-girls are perhaps looking for some garment—their presence in the picture being an excuse for the artist to create a sense of homeliness by means of what seems to be a workaday scene. Their gestures fairly vibrate in the light pouring in at the window, engendering a near-musical effect in the background, and enhancing the vital inner sparkle of Venus' nude body.

TITIAN

15

POPE PAUL III WITH HIS NEPHEWS ALESSANDRO AND OTTAVIO FARNESE

1546. Museo Nazionale di Capodimonte, Naples
Oil on canvas, 200 × 127 cm

Vasari states that the picture was commissioned by the Farnese family in Rome, 1546. Titian had arrived in Rome by the end of the year 1545 to be welcomed by Bembo, Cardinal Alessandro Farnese and Paul III himself. He had contacts with a number of artists, including Vasari, Sebastiano del Piombo and Michelangelo. About this time he painted several portraits, an *Ecce Homo*, and the *Danae* of Capodimonte for the Farnese family.

The triple portrait is clear evidence of his intention to portray the psychology of his human subjects. He both wishes and needs to make analytical and introspective investigation into the types of people he paints, and into customs in order to use them in a new representational mode of courtly art.

16

TITIAN

POPE PAUL III WITH HIS NEPHEWS ALESSANDRO AND OTTAVIO FARNESE (detail)

The features of the characters, their free and easy movements, rather rare in sixteenth-century portraiture, lend the picture qualities which are rich in human emotions. Indeed, with fresh and fluid brushwork the artist disclosed minute characteristics of the characters, yet, at the same time, opened up broad pictorial perspectives. This work is a veritable "Chorus of Portraits" and belongs to the most profound creations of Italian painting. Along with those fellow-artists worthy of him, Titian created pure synthesis without severing the links that connected him with the noblest traditions of Venetian painting. "At that time this art revolutionized the world to such an extent that neither Florence nor Rome were ever able to experience again a Classicism conceived in this way" (R. Longhi, 1946).

LORENZO LOTTO
c. 1480–1556

PORTRAIT OF A NOBLEMAN

About 1527. Gallerie dell'Accademia, Venice
Oil on canvas, 98 × 110 cm

In the artistic scene of sixteenth-century Venice, which was dominated by Titian, Lorenzo Lotto cuts a singular figure. Diametrically opposed to Giorgione's "tonal revolution", his brushwork is in fact thrown into relief by a certain chromatic intensity; his glittering colours do not blend into the overall tone of surrounding space. He exposes the anticlassical canon and, in his incisive depiction of reality, shows a strong influence of Antonello's drawing and Dürer's prints. His manner is accordingly subdued, quietly unrhetorical, a deliberate revolt against the Titianesque school of courtly art. It is also in character that he should take simple burghers and members of the petty nobility as his models instead of pontiffs and rulers. His portrayal of them is not realistic, he seeks to establish a dialogue, a tangible point of contact between himself and the model, thus creating what might pass as the earliest examples of psychologizing portraiture.

In this particular work, the model is caught in an unstable posture, a preamble to some gesture or fidgety movement, as if to signify inner uncertainty and unease. By far the most telling of this prolific artist's portraits, it is dipped, as it were, in a chilly light, which stresses the sharp edges of all the picture's components, from the human figure to the objects, so placed as to impart a kind of chromatic motion to the scene.

18

SEBASTIANO DEL PIOMBO
(SEBASTIANO LUCIANI OR FRA SEBASTIAN VINIZIAN)
c. 1485–1547

PORTRAIT OF A MAN

About 1515–20. Museum of Fine Arts, Budapest
Oil on wood, 115 × 94 cm

The Museum acquired the picture in 1895 through the intermediary of Károly Pulszky. Originally from Milan (first intimation 1644), it found its way into Prince Francesco I d'Este's collection (A. Venturi, 1882). Owned by the Modena writer Cerretti in 1797, the year 1808 saw it in Pavia, in the possession of Antonio Scarpa di Motta of Livenza.

Even when the collection came up for auction, experts were attributing the work to Raphael, the subject being identified as the poet Antonio Tebaldeo. The landscape in the background and the very depth of the light confer a Venetian touch and recall Giorgione. Presumably painted in Rome between 1515 and 1520, it bears the stamp of Sebastiano del Piombo's art. Distancing himself from the Giorgione influence, he increasingly aspired to the monumental, as witnessed by the positioning of the figure and the measured accuracy of architectural detail.

GIROLAMO SAVOLDO
c. 1480–after 1548

19

TOBIAS AND THE ANGEL

About 1540. Galleria Borghese, Rome
Oil on canvas, 96 × 126 cm

Acquired by the Gallery in 1911, the painting, after various attributions, was at last correctly assigned to Savoldo by Cantalamessa (1914), who thus put an end to the legend of Titian's authorship—a view held while the picture was housed in the Alfani Palace in Perugia.

Dating from around 1540 (De Logu, 1958), one of the most pregnant periods of the Brescian artist's lifework, it shows a certain kinship with the *St. Matthew* in the New York Metropolitan Museum.

"The most lyrical personality of the Brescia School . . . reared on complex formative influences combining Lombard-Veneto, Tuscan and Flemish elements . . . a blend that provides the key to this most solitary of figures in the sixteenth-century history of Northern Italian art" (Pallucchini).

In *Tobias and the Angel* there converge all the lines of his development as a painter, glazed over by his special visual concept of light. It is a knife-edged light that penetrates into the folds, turning shadows into colour. All is suffused with this mysterious coloured luminosity, conferring a quality of transparency and airiness upon the landscape and, more than anywhere, on the backdrop of trees in whose midst the figures linger or move, "a veil of dream hovering about the images plunged in silence" (A. Venturi).

GIROLAMO ROMANINO (DI ROMANO)
c. 1484/87–1562

20

PORTRAIT OF A NOBLEMAN

1515–20. Museum of Fine Arts, Budapest
Oil on canvas, 82.5 × 71.5 cm

The painting originates from the Fenaroli Collection of Brescia. It was bought by Károly Pulszky in 1895 for the Budapest Museum from Luigi Resimini in Venice as a work by Moretto. Connoisseurs later decided that Romanino was the artist. A superb portrait, with wide sweeps of colour giving it force-fulness and majesty. This approach shows the artist wedded to the fresco style of dynamic brushwork covering large expanses in one colour. A. Venturi says (1928), in agreement, that "the soft modelling and the as yet unfrag-mented drawing place it in the years suggested". The vast tonal composition does not blur the accurately observed romantic and melancholy traits, which are the poignant marks of the inwardness of a probably complex character. A later replica at the Accademia Carrara in Bergamo shows a close resemblance to the magnificent Budapest portrait.

ALESSANDRO BONVICINO (MORETTO)
Brescia, c. 1498–1554

21

A SAINT

1530. Museum of Fine Arts, Budapest
Oil on wood, 81 × 71.5 cm

Acquired by Károly Pulszky for the Museum in 1895 it was at first held to be by Moroni. Frizzoni traced it to Moretto in 1903. The subject is alternately designated as St. Louis and St. Placid. The martyr-saint is placed as in a portrait, even though everything else seems to point to a fragment of an altarpiece. The very position of the figure, the drapery on the right, which adumbrates a corresponding one on the left, with, in the centre, a Madonna against the background of a typical Veneto scenery, would appear to suggest a work of Venetian inspiration, such as can be seen in Tosio Martinengo of Brescia's altar-piece of St. Anthony of Padua. His richly "atmospheric" Venetian colour scheme in particular bears witness to yet another attempt of his to test the tonal gamut. This is the particular moment in time that marks the birth of Moretto's true art at the confluence of Venetian painting and Brescian milieu, stamped by Moroni's, Romanino's and Savoldo's work, and seminal to an alternating pattern of fabulous colouring shot through with the cachets of "the radical tradition of Lombardy" (De Logu, 1958).

22

GIOVANNI BATTISTA MORONI
1520/30?–1578

PORTRAIT OF JACOPO FOSCARINI (?)

1575. Museum of Fine Arts, Budapest
Oil on canvas, 105 × 83.5 cm

The picture was in various Viennese collections until 1779. Count Zichy presented it to the City of Budapest in 1906. In 1953, it falled to the Museum of Fine Arts. The identity inscribed on the portrait—"Jacobus Contareno Potestas Paduae ... Aetatis ... G.B."—has been challenged, in that there was no Paduan burgomaster of that name about this time, the office being held by Jacopo Foscarini between 15th August, 1574 and 1st January, 1576. Be that as it may, there is every reason to agree with Berenson that "the personages portrayed by Moroni are anecdotal figures rather than specimens of humanity". At the most, therefore, it may pass for an honest and balanced portrait made on commission, whatever there is about it that is grandiose deriving, as Garas suggests, from the Venetian manner. The very type of portrait it represents, with the person portrayed placed in a setting of greyish architecture, is redolent of famous archetypes by Moretto.

JACOPO TINTORETTO (JACOPO ROBUSTI)
1518–1594

23

ST. MARK RESCUING A SLAVE

1548. Gallerie dell'Accademia, Venice
Oil on canvas, 416×544 cm

Originally in the Chapter Hall of the Scuola Grande di San Marco, the picture was spirited to Paris by the French in 1797, then given back to Venice where, with the Scuola closed, it found its final resting-place in the Gallery of the Academy.

As Ridolfi explains, the painting represents the miraculous intervention of St. Mark, who descends from Heaven to free a Provençal knight's slave, punished by his master with having "his eyes gouged out and his legs broken" for leaving the house unattended in order to visit the relics of the revered saint. The figure on the left is supposed to be Tommaso Rangone, Warden of the "School", who commissioned the other paintings at his own expense.

The painting caused not a few polemics, and led to arguments even among the patrons of the Scuola di San Marco, so much so that Tintoretto apparently went off with it in a huff, and only returned it in answer to pressing entreaties. Obviously enough, the novel idiom, both in form and colouring, embodied by this picture was bound, as Ridolfi remarks, to take the average viewer aback even though the Veneto compositional approach must be perfectly clear to the initiated eye. A. Venturi praises its "lithe power" and its "massive mechanism", and recalls Michelangelo and Titian with regard to Tintoretto's inventiveness in architecture and the foreshortening of human figures.

JACOPO TINTORETTO

24

ARIADNE, VENUS AND BACCHUS

1576. Doges' Palace, Anticollegio Hall, Venice
Oil on canvas, 146 × 167 cm

One of a set of four allegories painted by Tintoretto at the age of 60, and finished in 1577. Called *Vulcan's Workshop with the Cyclops*, *Mercury and the Graces*, *Pallas Sending away Mars* and *Ariadne, Venus and Bacchus*, the paintings were meant by the author to extol the unity and glory of the Venetian Republic. As Ridolfi construes it, Ariadne—discovered by Bacchus on the island of Naxos and crowned by Venus to be received amongst the gods—stands for Venice, born on the sea, graced by divine favour and crowned by freedom. In Tolnay's view, the imagery suggests the mythical marriage of Venice with the sea.

ARIADNE, VENUS AND BACCHUS (detail)

However one may interpret it, the composition is "admirable in its flowing mass of amber yellow, so light as to seem ethereal; perfect nude bodies appear, with light shining on them and vibrating, as if it came from an inexhaustible fountain; a harmonious rhythm of curves accompanies the alternation of light and shade, from which springs motion against the unending blue of sky and sea . . ." (Lorenzetti, 1926).

JACOPO TINTORETTO

26

THE LAST SUPPER

1592–94. Church of San Giorgio Maggiore, Venice
Oil on canvas, 365 × 568 cm

The artist used the subject repeatedly, this particular Last Supper being the definitive, and the most grandiose version. Tintoretto worked on this painting and on the *Fall of the Manna* on the opposite wall, during the last two years of his life. As his collaborators contributed little, the forcefulness radiating from this at once realistic and visionary creation is all the more astounding. The elongated shadows of the human figures, the ectoplasmic shapes of angels looming forth into view out of the smoke-dimmed halo of the lamps, the tensely-quivering rapport between the several scenes—everything is calculated to imbue the whole with "an all but expressionist feeling" (Pallucchini).

"The illusionary effect of a rotating table, the chiaroscuro contrasts between light and shade, the smooth flow and the abrupt shattering of lines, the grating of the colours—all this combines to generate this highly-strung feeling of intense movement, this hallucinatory vision contrasting and mutually complementing the real with the unreal, the physical with the metaphysical" (Coletti, 1944).

27

PAOLO VERONESE (CALIARI)
1528–1588

THE FEAST AT THE HOUSE OF LEVI

1573. Gallerie dell'Accademia, Venice
Oil on canvas, 1280 × 550 cm

Art criticism has always devoted special attention to this work: Boschini, Lanzi, Zanetti, Gauthier, Venturi, Fiocco, Pallucchini and De Logu have all ranked it as one of Paolo Veronese's *chefs-d'œuvre*.

Bearing unchallengeable testimony to the most orthodox principles of the philosophy of art, it provides a moral document and an accurate reassertion of aesthetic values as opposed to the customary narrative conception.

It was commissioned by Father Andrea Buono for the Church of SS. Giovanni e Paolo, to be hung in the friars' refectory.

Following shortly on the great "Feast" of Monteberico, it places the figures, similarly, within the framework of architectonic structures. As Ridolfi put it (1648), "the scene below a spacious loggia built of three wide arches commands a view of fine buildings and palaces".

An imaginary scene no doubt, but there is also a clear intention of using it to convey the rather vague ideas the artist had conceived of how to infuse fresh blood into Venetian architecture. In the same way as Carpaccio in his paintings of St. Ursula, Veronese adopts the architectural forms and concepts of his day, which is also the age of Sansovino, Palladio and Sanmicheli.

The table companions are seated as on a stage, arranged according to a co-ordinated plan under a canon of painting that seeks to fill the gaps in the architecture. "The many-stranded unfolding of the happenings is projected against the fantastic backcloth of the buildings" (Pallucchini, 1939).

28

PAOLO VERONESE

THE FEAST AT THE HOUSE OF LEVI (detail)

The perfectly natural and precisely-calculated effects of the scene brought on Veronese an accusation from the Holy Office of the Inquisition. The charge against him was that he had peopled the setting with soldiers, dogs and buffoons—with a "castle" which, in those days, was denied of citizens— within religious iconography. In his defence he pleaded that his endeavour had merely been to depict history in the picturesque terms of painting. "This is superb art—where the monumental grandeur of the vision is veiled over with a cold and airy-light haze. Paolo has written a new page in the book of profound humanity—the humanity and freedom of art" (De Logu). To this his rejoinder to the Inquisitor witnessed: "I make my pictures with proper care, to the very utmost of which my understanding is capable."

A compromise was then agreed, with the artist changing the name of the painting and drawing on St. Luke's Gospel (5, 29): "And Levi made him a grand feast in his own house: and there was a great company of publicans and of others that sat down with them."

This earned him an acquittal and saved the painting, adding this novel and so far undreamt-of image to the iconography of holy feasts.

PAOLO VERONESE

THE RAPE OF EUROPA

1576–1580. Doges' Palace, Anticollegio Hall, Venice
Oil on canvas, 240 × 303 cm

29

Painted between 1576 and 1580, the picture was reported by Zanetti as hanging in its present place in 1733; it was removed by the French in 1797 and taken to Paris, where it was restored and altered. It represents the mythical rape of Europa by Jupiter in the guise of a bull, as she prepares to mount on the god's back with the help of her maids. The action unfolds towards the right in the manner of a stage sequence, in successive scenes down to the final plunge into the waves of the sea. The composition clearly marks the moment of transition from Renaissance Classicism to seventeenth-century Arcadia. The sumptuous décor and rich colouring were to provide a seminal experience for subsequent Baroque painting. Thus the painting initiates the exaltation of the ruling class through court mythology intended to rekindle the aristocracy's love of pomp and circumstance by allegories with which it could identify itself.

PAOLO VERONESE

30

THE APOTHEOSIS OF VENICE

c. 1583. Doges' Palace, Hall of the Great Council, Venice
Oil on canvas, 904 × 508 cm

After the fire of 1577, the ceiling of the Hall was rebuilt by Cristoforo Sorte between 1578 and 1585. The repainting was done by Veronese, Tintoretto and Palma the Younger. Veronese painted the oval which shows the triumph of Venice crowned with victory under Doge Niccolò da Ponte. While the work was enthusiastically received by contemporary writers, modern art criticism has reappraised its worth and has pointed out the artificiality of its glorificatory intent. This, however, detracts nothing from the merits of the compositional structure and the pictorial texture, in spite of the rather heavy alterations. The initial freshness can be clearly seen in the original pen-sketch on dark paper with white highlights (Earl of Harewood's collection). Here again the authorities are the main protagonists, swamped by symbols and images of classical mythology, with the gods above and the aristocracy below, dressed in the same sumptuous raiment. The balustrade in the middle carries the coat of arms of the Doge, and this recurs repeatedly on the carvings of the cornices.

JACOPO DA PONTE (IL BASSANO)
c. 1515–1592

31

THE SUPPER AT EMMAUS

About 1538. Cittadella, Sacristy of the Parish Church
Oil on canvas, 235 × 250 cm

Although undated, the painting is likely to go back to about 1538, a particularly felicitous period in Jacopo Bassano's art.

Lorenzetti (1911) places it in the early part of the artist's stay in Bonifazio da Pitati's workshop and pointed out the obvious links with the latter's painting on the same theme, now to be seen in the Brera. There is a certain contrast between the solemn, hieratic figure of Christ and the rough and realistic close-up of the innkeeper on the one hand, and on the other, the little scene of the crouching dog being teased by the cat from a distance (Zampetti, 1957). The postures of the two disciples, the laboured perspective of the table, and some genre episodes were to recur in his later "Supper" version, now in the Borghese Gallery, Rome (E. Arslan, 1960).

The still-life in the centre of the work standing but against the linen table-cloth is a marvel of pictorial observation. A virtually lone harbinger of the main marks and elements of forthcoming Venetian painting (Tintoretto), Jacopo Bassano here sweeps the scene clear.

In any case, light is the master here; it picks out the details and throws them into sharp outline.

DOMENICO FETTI
1589–1624

32

DAVID

Gallerie dell'Accademia, Venice
Oil on canvas, 174×130 cm

The work was donated to the Gallerie by the Contarinis in 1838. Fetti made repeated use of the subject of David. Two other versions of the subject are to be found in Dresden and in the Viezzoli Collection in Genoa.

An innovator—together with Liss and Strozzi—of early seventeenth-century Venetian painting, Fetti was clearly influenced by Caravaggio in this work. He arrived in Venice in 1621 and died there two years later. In this short time he painted the series of fine *Parables*, in which he managed " ... to fuse Caravaggio's world and the Veneto universe; in these paintings the light, moving unfettered and increasingly restlessly, loosens up Caravaggio's powerful chromatic substance to the point of ultimately dissolving and eroding it to the utmost" (Michelini, *Arte Veneta*, 1955).

Here again it is light that takes over, light instinct with touches of Lombard and Roman feeling, and fleshy, soft Rubensian brushwork that moves freely in setting this youth in the colour-scheme as "more than a figure of myth —with the attributes of a man of his time—rather than of the victor of Goliath the giant". Thus, with inventive freedom and freshness of vision, Fetti envelops any subject, profane or religious, with the warmth of human sympathy (Valcanover, 1960).

33

JAN LISS (PAN)
c. 1595–1629

VENUS IN FRONT OF THE MIRROR

1625/26. Galleria degli Uffizi, Florence
Oil on canvas, 83 × 69 cm

Reared in the Dutch and Flemish school, a disciple of Hendrick Goltzius, Liss absorbed a wide variety of experiences in his youth; he acquired at the Haarlem school his zest for the popular approach to portraiture, with glowing colours and firmly clean-cut forms.

Coming to Venice in 1621, he probably met Fetti, whose influence mellowed his painting and made for more richly-modulated colouring and light. The material has a fresh look, and is edged with "frills", thus ushering in the first dawning of the Baroque in Venice.

The *Venus* is a product of the artist's maturity from his Venetian period, which saw his attention turning from the genre scene towards themes of mythological inspiration. The sway and spell of his predecessors' artistry, in particular that of Veronese, as bred by the Venetian milieu is still there; but there is also a foretaste of that bucolic mythologizing which was a prelude to Sebastiano Ricci's pictorial "symphonies". The work is a link, then not only in the world of Venetian art, but in the painting of the whole of Central Europe.

34

BERNARDO STROZZI
1581–1644

THE CHARITY OF ST. LAWRENCE

1639/40. San Niccolò da Tolentino, Venice
Oil on canvas, 206 × 162 cm

From the very outset, Strozzi broke with the traditional Genoese manner, welcoming the new Flemish touch and Rubens' innovations, whence his relish for rankly lush, thickly meaty brushwork. He arrived in Venice about 1630 and enriched his palette still further by adopting Veronese's predilection for blazing and sparkling colouring. "His colour-scheme brightens into a spontaneously buoyant luminosity" (Pallucchini).

The Charity of St. Lawrence can be dated to the first period of the artist's stay in Venice, in that some violent chiaroscuro effects and a certain gusto in the handling of the material show him still close to the Genoese phase. There is a demonstrable influence of Rubens in the figure of the child sprawled on the ground. The sensuous and massive brushwork is carried almost to excess. The composition of the subject-matter, which the artist reformulated time and again, is given a new form. Within a correct balance of distinctively Venetian pictorial "quantities", the painting is built up on the balance between an open-air scene and the inner drive and movement of the composition with the lines converging from the outside inwards, to the focal point of the entire work, as "conveyed by the widened-out horizon and the soft cadences" (Mortari, 1966).

35

SEBASTIANO RICCI
c. 1659–1734

THE ASSUMPTION (sketch)

1733. Museum of Fine Arts, Budapest
Oil on canvas, 95 × 51.5 cm

Ricci's work is a realization of differing pictorial and compositional endeavours. Steeped in the Venetian environment, he joined the ranks of those painters who followed up the line of late-17th-century local painting. He blazed a trail in retracing his steps to the very wellhead of the great tradition of post-Renaissance Venetian art in general, and within it, the particular artist most congenial to him, Paolo Veronese (Zampetti, 1969).

The Budapest sketch of *The Assumption* of the Virgin dates back to shortly before the great altar-piece for the Vienna Karlskirche was carried out in 1733–34, not long before his death.

Some further variants are the sketches at Melnik (Czechoslovakia) and at Aschaffenburg.

The work is most likely the one found in his room at his death, as established by the "inventory of his effects".

The composition is transformed into a wavy spiral design of the kind he would use in altar paintings. The hotly vivid colours and the breezy, animated brushwork ascend in vaporous flights of paint, as though to peg the idea in the very first flush of its conception. He succeeds in all this with the supreme ease and immediacy that mark the vitality of his genius down to the very last phase of his versatile and prolific lifework.

MARCO RICCI
1676–1729

36

LANDSCAPE WITH A MOUNTAIN BROOK, MONKS AND OTHER FIGURES

About 1720. Gallerie dell'Accademia, Venice
Canvas, 136 × 197 cm

This picture was restored by A. Lazzarin in 1963. It was previously in the possession of the Corniani Algarotti Gallery in Treviso, then of Countess Perazzolo. It was purchased by Count Zanetti in Venice in 1878.

It is the counterpart of the painting *Landscape with Watering Horses*. Both are fairly well-known works, dating from about 1720. In the background of the latter the valley of the River Piave is depicted. Generally, this picture is considered to be one of Marco Ricci's masterpieces.

The artist had a harassed life of hardship trailing off to a sad end, if the chroniclers—rather than the critics—are to be believed. Apprenticed to his uncle Sebastiano, he savoured the ferment of new stirrings in the world of Venetian art. It brought forth in him a narrative streak in what was just then fairly taking over the Venetian art scene—landscape painting. Drinking in the Flemish Tempesta's landscapes, Magnasco's vibrant artistry, all that he saw and assimilated on his frequent travels alone and with his uncle he converted, in an intense and many-sided creative zeal, into forms all his own. Pallucchini and Valcanover (1951, 1955) admit "the difficulty, to this day, of reconstructing Marco Ricci's art, in view of the total lack of data". Though Goering's chronology had been lengthy and cumbersome enough, Ivanoff (Emporium, 1948) included in it this picture, too, for he considered it the beginning of a trend leading from the chiaroscuro style of the Baroque towards the colourful light effects of the eighteenth century. Later, in 1957, Pallucchini stated that these light effects were inevitable in view of Ricci's links with the countryside. The historian Zanetti mentioned (*Della pitture venetiana . . .*, Venice, 1771, p. 573) that like a "pilgrim", Ricci used to return to the region of Belluno, where he found ideas for his painting and matured his new techniques. The picture itself portrays the sense of the place (Pallucchini, *Pittura veneziana del Settecento*, Rome, 1960, p. 39, fig. 96), by the unbroken, atmospheric flow of light, which makes the chiaroscuro verticals of the group of trees even more striking. This new susceptibility was nothing more than a novel approach to reality, which sprung out of the shadow of the rhetoric which had preceded it. It almost seems as if the light itself enjoyed setting off the figures in the foreground while harmonically inundating the background. Yes, here lies a new pictorial approach.

GIOVANNI BATTISTA PIAZZETTA
1682–1754

37

THE FORTUNE-TELLER

1740. Gallerie dell'Accademia, Venice
Oil on canvas, 154×114 cm

His father brought him up to the wood-carver's craft, which was trying hard to provide a kind of "poor man's" sequel to the heroic sculpture of the preceding century.

He entered the world of painters with Zanchi and later with Molinari where his art took on greater depth, sensitivity, and variety of style. He spent the subsequent years, along with other Veneto artists, at the Bologna school of Crespi, the real, forceful master of the new style.

The year 1711 found him back in Venice, his home city, where he brought back the new moods and trends, and perfected his painting skill. He had by now arrived at a more realistic new vision governed by the prevalent chiaroscuro, the harbinger of the concept of form that was to culminate in a brilliant highlighting of colour. His sensuous brushwork feeds on a palette dipped in velvety greys and burnt browns, with the undiluted chromatic values of the bright tints standing out against them like flashes of light. *The Fortune-Teller* in the Galleries of the Accademia is from his mature period, as witnessed by the notice on the back of the picture, which reads: "This is the epitaph of the famous painter Piazzetta, who made this painting ordered from him in Venice in 1740, and was paid fifteen gold ducats for it" (Fiocco). The work is of supreme importance for an understanding of the artist's development, placing him as it does among the great precursors of eighteenth-century Franco-European taste (De Logu, 1958).

The layout, with the "imposing popular figure" dominating the whole, is made pyramidal by the placing of the other persons and the spiralling movement of their gestures. The copiously-stippled play of greys and pinks set off against the reddish brown and dark green of the background turns the canvas into "a shining light that gives coherence to all the components of the colour scheme, bordering them with a foamlike effect that manages to convey the very stirring of the air" (Pallucchini, 1956). There is also a vague reminder of his Emilian heritage brought away from Crespi's school, which imparts to this painting, in its compositional endeavour, and still more in its chromatic values, a certain kinship with the woman lute-player in the Paris Vitale Bloch Collection—a work he might well have seen during his pupilage at Crespi's. Be that as it may, this affinity underlines his attachment to that accurate Emilian naturalism which he knew how to weave so well into the subsequent Venetian colour context.

GIOVANNI BATTISTA TIEPOLO
1696–1770

38

THE GLORY OF SPAIN

1764. Madrid Royal Palace, ceiling of the Throne Room
Fresco, 27 × 10 m

G.B. Tiepolo, whose "order-book" in his big workshop was always over-flowing with commissions, appears as something of a painter-contractor, delivering himself of a stream of productions with a sense of tradition, an adherence to what has survived of a "glorious" past.

Such a scene possibly lived only in the mind of the artist, and not in that of his powerful patrons. Tiepolo went to Madrid with the sketch for this ceiling fresco already completed back in Venice. Contributing a great deal to this impressive work were his two sons Gian Domenico and Lorenzo, to help their 66-year-old father who suffered greatly because of the tiring journey. But their contribution was stylistically attuned to the father's unitary conception and perfectly adapted itself to its manner and mannerisms.

The moulding of the lower part of the ceiling features an encomium of Charles III's virtues: above this cornice, groups of people from Spain's possessions alternate with figures and animals from all parts. The historical episodes are enriched by outlandish extravagance in the detail. Floating as in a whirlpool in the centre of the heavens are clusters of the Virtues, mythical beings, gods, cupids—the whole repertory of Tiepolo's themes—gathered together in celebration of the dynasty and its power. Nevertheless, the design "shows a congruous alignment of the separate elements. The void that gapes in the centre, snapping the spiral girdle of the composition at different points, is the real subject of the work" (Mariuz, 1972).

One can merely conjecture how the concluding phase of Venetian painting had arrived at an "epilogue" (if that is the right word) of this sort; set apart from the general context of the great Roman Baroque by its inherent Venetian-ness alone, it has penetrated to all Central Europe by virtue of Tiepolo's contributions.

GIOVANNI BATTISTA TIEPOLO

39

THE APOSTLE ST. JAMES THE GREATER CONQUERING THE MOORS

1757. Museum of Fine Arts, Budapest
Oil on canvas, 317 × 163 cm

After the ceilings of the Royal Palace in Madrid, Tiepolo was commissioned to do six altar-pieces for the convent of Aranjuez; they were subsequently removed to make way for canvases in the neo-Classical manner on the advice of the King's confessor, Father Electa, who preferred the new style imported to Spain by Mengs.

Morassi maintains (1962) that this picture, as well as those of the cycle referred to, was destined for the same convent; Anna Pallucchini in her turn advances the hypothesis that the work, done in Venice for the Spanish Ambassador in London and mentioned by Gradenigo (Notatorii), obviously mistakenly, as a St. George, was completed in Madrid.

In any case the canvas dates to the years 1757–58, and may well claim the highest prestige among the master's altar-pieces. The plot, as Garas (1961) points out, moves on two different levels, both clearly influenced by Veronese. One, with strictly conventional imagery, is "all lapped by a wash of silvery-pearly colours" (Morassi), the other, in the background, is boldly foreshortened to confer spaciousness on the historical narrative.

The arrangement might well suggest a draft for a small ceiling rather than an altar-piece, so typical is it of Tiepolo's manner of pictorial layout. That is obviously what the upward-from-below position of the figure is designed to convey, in particular that of the Saint's head, the soaring of the banner into the wide open celestial spaces—all essential ingredients of his decorative formula. Yet here these features are merged in order to develop the basic compositional concept—a harking back to the standard "design" of the altar-piece executed by the time-honoured canons of the art.

GIAN DOMENICO TIEPOLO
1727–1804

40

THE PROMENADE

1791. Museo Correr (Ca' Rezzonico), Venice
Detail of the stripped fresco from the Villa Zianigo at Mira
200 × 150 cm

Here Gian Domenico reverts to the treatment of composition which his father brought to a similar scene in the Villa Valmarana near Monteberico (dated to 1737 by De Logu, 1757 by Morassi). But here he amplifies the original conception into a wider view in keeping with his own enlarged horizon, shifting things on to a new plane of visual perspective. Broad expanses of hazy brown set off the vivid figures from the cold hues of the surroundings. "Gian Domenico moves these images into close contact with their setting, lodging them, like other 'paternal archetypes' of his, in an empirical space" (Mariuz, 1972).

The scenes from life represented appear under a new and novel aspect of landscape and environment.

The elegant lady promenading on the arms of her husband and beau is also accompanied by her favourite lap dog held by a man servant. It is the artist's clear intention to achieve verisimilitude in the portrayal of people and things.

41

ROSALBA CARRIERA
1675–1757

PORTRAIT OF A LADY

Gallerie dell'Accademia, Venice
Pastel on cardboard, 57 × 47 cm

The artist was an attractive and outstanding practitioner of the so-called minor arts, which flourished in Venice in the eighteenth century. In the beginning she painted miniatures but she soon concentrated on the pastel technique and became a portraitist of European renown. She was elected member of the Academies, first of Rome, and then of Venice. In addition to commissions from the Italian nobility she was overwhelmed with invitations to foreign countries and also scored great successes in Paris and in Vienna. This pastel portrait, which belonged to the Royal Collection in Venice before being transferred to the Galleries of the Accademia, had mistakenly been considered the likeness of Rosalba Carriera herself. The distinguished and haughty lady, attired in laces and furs, with a conspicuous mole on her face, is obviously not the painter, as can be easily proved by a comparison with her self-portraits (cf. Malamani, *Bolletino d'Arte* 1928/29).
Under the magic of the painter's touch, graceful and airy and yet penetrating the depths of the sitter's character, the unknown lady appears as a typical representative of the Venice of her period. R. Longhi's apt words (1946), refer to Rosalba's peerless talent for characterization: "With an incomparable power Rosalba could express the airy delicacy of her period."

PIETRO LONGHI (PIETRO FALCA)
1702–1785

42

HUNTING IN THE LAGOON

About 1760. Pinacoteca Querini Stampalia, Venice
Oil on canvas, 57 × 74 cm

Pietro Longhi was first a pupil of Balestra and then of Crespi whose art was the source of his realism, which expressed a sober and sincere inner world, and a delight in detailed and fresh narrative. He conveyed his realism with wit and ease, whereas the immediacy with which he approached the landscape enriched his painting with a unique quality. Up to a certain point these elements can be discerned in pre-revolution French painting (Watteau, Chardin, Boucher and Lancret), whose influence also made itself felt in Pietro Longhi's Realism. Only here and there did grotesque features appear in his art; he saw his figures with the eye of a sage and a gentle and witty impertinence is to be found in many of the scenes he depicted.

Pietro Longhi became, by means of his genre-painting, one of the most faithful chroniclers of his age, and one who conjured up a regrettably vanished civilization (Pignatti, 1968). It should be borne in mind, however, that his connection with Goldoni and the teachings of Emilia encouraged him, through the observation of reality, to perform a kind of analysis of "social depths"; he did not want to cause an upheaval but only wanted to point out—perhaps tendentiously—the ineptitude of a declining class of society. Although he did not pass sentence, he allowed his opinion to be known, being fully aware that changes were ineminent. Sometimes he would ironically represent certain dandies, abbots and virgins. *Hunting in the Lagoon* was a product of a period of renewal in his style, although in his picture "he returned to a clear theme, unfolded with exquisite shades" (Pignatti, 1968) in broad surfaces and brownish tones. As always, here too, the description is accurate. In the preparatory drawing (Correr, No. 475) he had outlined his ideas, which were then realized in the airy painting. He recorded the world of the lagoons at the exact moment of the hunt, depicting with particular detail the bow, from which small terracotta marbles and not arrows were shot. The widespread use of these marbles has been revealed by recent explorations in the lagoons; hitherto this form of hunting had been unknown.

According to Giulio Lorenzetti (1934) the hunter represented with the arrow was a member of the Barbarigo family.

A very short time ago a variant, very similar to our present picture and corresponding to No. 476 of the Correr list, was discovered (London, O'Nian Gallery), (Pignatti, 1968).

43

ALESSANDRO LONGHI
1733–1813

PORTRAIT OF JACOPO GRADENIGO

1778–1781. Museo Civico, Padua
Oil on canvas, 233 × 137 cm

Pignatti found out the name of the sitter, as well as the office he held in 1948. Jacopo Gradenigo occupied various positions but it seems probable that the portrait was painted at the time when he was chief admiral, for the city visible in the background was found to be Corfu, the seat of the holder of this office. This opinion is supported by the sitter's age, which corresponds with the time during which he held this position.

The arrangement is that of an official portrait: the naval officer standing in a haughty posture, with a hardly noticeable smile on his lips, holds his admiral's baton and faces the painter. But Longhi avoids the purely professional approach and offers instead a colour symphony of red and gold, of pale and vivid hues; he reveals, too, in the likeness his own ironical aloofness. He was introduced to the craft of painting by his father; he later became a pupil of Giuseppe Nogari but was to some extent also influenced by Piazzetta. The decisive part of his œuvre was portraiture, in which he "proved to be a unique and outstanding personality" (De Logu, 1958). His figures, in addition to official portraiture, show a certain malice, reflecting subtle Venetian satire.

GIOVANNI ANTONIO CANAL (CANALETTO)
1697–1768

44

THE RIALTO BRIDGE (DETAIL)

Galleria Nazionale, Rome
Oil on canvas, 68.5 × 92 cm

His father, the eminent painter of stage scenery, introduced this artist to his own craft and then to painting in general. Later he became one of the greatest representatives of the numerous eminent *vedutists* which the eighteenth century produced. However, in contrast to the others, he wanted to present a picture, and one as faithful as possible, of the Venice of his time. He did not use his dexterity and craftsmanship as ends in themselves, but considered them means by which reality could be expressed most scientifically. To prove this, it is enough to consider how the painter, the faithful interpreter of the culture of European enlightenment, utilized the *camera obscura* in order to correct possible mistakes to which the eye had become accustomed by Baroque perspective.

However, side by side with this trend another one, usually called genre-painting, also appeared, in this movement insignificant episodes were depicted with outstanding clearsightedness and bearing the hallmark of the new pictorial approach. This style had its initiators both in the world of the lagoons and on the mainland, among them Luca Carlevaris of Udine, Michele Marieschi, Gabriele Bella and Bernardino Bisson.

Canaletto's pictorial art was the last evidence of the political greatness of Venice, which he proudly presented to the European (and chiefly to the English) public. His serene aspect was consciously based upon values of colours and of light. His canvases are simply overwhelmed with light and colours and this powerful vibration sets off, with crystal-clearness, landscapes and edifices in front of a confused background.

The Rialto Bridge, which, along with so many other pictures of his, were once attributed to Bellotto, is an organic part of his œuvre and is now definitely considered to be his work. Recent cleaning has revealed the original pictorial formulation of the picture; its novelty lies in the very fact that it is completely comprehensible.

BERNARDO BELLOTTO (CANALETTO)
1720–1780

45

THE KAUNITZ PALACE AND GARDEN IN VIENNA

1759–60. Museum of Fine Arts, Budapest
Oil on canvas, 134×237 cm

Even during their own lifetime confusion reigned concerning the two artists' names, when attempts were made to identify the sitter and the works.
Bellotto, too, travelled widely and followed the compulsory course of the Venetian *vedutists*; he belonged to the vigorous group of so-called foreigners, who not only continued the style but indicated with their activity how culture was animatedly advancing within exactly demarcated limits. He certainly inherited from his uncle the awareness that a new reality, the objective vision of optical reality, was to be created in a picture.
This Bellotto was by then a weary and inferior successor to a much more lively tradition. The picture in question is unnaturally rigid and it represents, in all probability, the palace of the powerful Chancellor, Prince Kaunitz. The picture belonged to the series in which Bellotto depicted the *vedute* of Viennese palaces for Maria Theresa. As in so many other cases, here too, he was helped by Torelli or another artist in painting the figures, which look like puppets and clash with the harmony of their surroundings and nature.

FRANCESCO ZUCCARELLI
1702–1778

46

BULL-HUNTING

About 1736. Gallerie dell'Accademia, Venice
Oil on canvas, 114 × 150 cm

Although clever Zuccarelli was fond of landscapes he always had a slight nostalgia for portraiture. In vain was he stunted and distorted, in vain was he enclosed in his isolation, in vain was this longing suppressed by the freer, fresher and more fluid talent of the born landscape painter; he stood out from among the mass of his fellow artists. He had a talent, rare among landscape painters for portraiture, too. He began his studies in Florence and Rome and then came under the influence of Venice and of Ricci. It was during this period (1732–1751) that he painted his best pictures of the lagoons.

Bull-Hunting is connected with a trend akin to Central European or rather French culture (Boucher and Fragonard), in which mythological and Arcadian representations (landscapes and customs) were virtually "compulsory". This seems to have been the cultural trend of the period, a culture conveyed by channels that, although not of Italian origin, clearly revealed the deep feelings of the age. The starting-point of the picture is the game of the same name, which took place on the piazza in front of San Polo. Documentary art was the artist's speciality, and accordingly, setting out from this open-air game, he represented his theme in nature, idyllically and, at the same time, solemnly, for this was the subject with which he could display his gifts best.

47

GIANANTONIO AND FRANCESCO GUARDI
1699–1760 and 1712–1793

MADONNA AND CHILD WITH ST. ANTHONY THE ABBOT, ST. DOMINIC, ST. SEBASTIAN AND ST. MARK

Belvedere di Aquileia (Udine), Parish Church of Antonio Abate
Oil on embroidered canvas, 234 × 154 cm

In eighteenth-century Venetian painting there reigned a family, a veritable dynasty of painters. Their art, which was partly defined by critics to be "in minore", united allegorical and mythological trends with new, animated and ardent passions and endowed *vedute* painting with new qualities, in fact with a new "Impressionism", which gave it a new impetus.

The altar-piece of Belvedere, commissioned by Savorgnan (as is evinced by the coat of arms at the feet of the Madonna's throne) is of outstanding importance, for it strictly defines Gianantonio's style and his amazing pictorial fantasy.

It was already Fogolari (1916) who commented on this picture with such emphasis as to make it later a part of Guardi's œuvre. This is what he wrote: "A swift milling of figures, lines and colours is in contrast to all rules of composition and of correct rhythm; yet it displays so much taste, ardour and dash that it causes joy and delight . . . the artist has a singular method of abolishing strict shapes with a view to creating an enchanting mistiness."

After the 1965 Guardi exhibition in Venice Zampetti (in the catalogue) recognized, on grounds of earlier indications, the "peerless severity of Gianantonio's style". The airy altar-piece of the glorious Madonna is full of colouristic emotions produced by a conscious and impetuous handling of the canvas. The tones appear with a tempestuous swiftness, they blend, they show nuances, they softly model every figure and they present gentle outlines. Sure and significant connections make themselves felt with the celebrating angels of the Church of Angelo Raffaele. The contour elements are strikingly similar in the angels strewing flowers at the top and in the putto at the bottom of the throne.

FRANCESCO GUARDI
1712–1792

48

GONDOLA IN THE LAGOON

1765–70. Museo Poldi Pezzoli, Milan
Oil on canvas, 25 × 38 cm

Francesco Guardi was a collaborator of Gianantonio, from whom he learned the craft of painting, but he introduced into his older brother's art his own profoundly meditative personality. This fact is evinced by the essential differences to be discerned in the works the "workshop" produced.

This picture, unanimously attributed by researchers to Francesco, is, in all likelihood, the fragment of a larger composition. The whole scene is summarized in the slow and calm movement of the gondoliere in the foreground, whereas the scenery of the lagoon virtually disintegrates in the mother-of-pearl atmosphere, which is lightened here and there by some rare flashes in the background.

The emotional intensity of the painting is condensed into this brief recording of the moment, as if it were a "phrase in music", for example in Vivaldi's or Albinoni's compositions of the same theme. The smooth lagoon and the *adagio continuo* are parallel motifs of picture and music. The scenery becomes dissolved in musicality, as musicality disintegrates "in sorrowful weeping" (Goethe).

"The mournful character of the black gondola" is both a forecast and a conscious experience of the future destiny of the world of lagoons—a world enclosed within its own modest boundaries. This is a world which has disappeared, because it was linked to a declining civilization.

The argument was not continued, and it has not been taken up again; the other lagoon painters, such as the members of the Burano school, could not disguise the emptiness—not only of form but also of content.